Growing
in
Remarriage

Growing in Remarriage

Seven Keys to a Successful Second Marriage

Jim Smoke

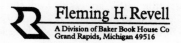

Fleming H. Revell
A Division of Baker Book House Co
Grand Rapids, Michigan 49516

© 1990 by Jim Smoke

Published by Fleming H. Revell
a division of Baker Book House Company
P.O. Box 6287, Grand Rapids, MI 49516-6287

First paperback edition 1994

Printed in the United States of America

Library of Congress Cataloging-in-Publication Data

Smoke, Jim.
    Growing in remarriage / Jim Smoke.
      p. cm.
    Includes bibliography references.
    ISBN 0-8007-5523-5
    1. Remarried people—Religious life. 2. Remarriage—Religious aspects—Christianity. 3. Divorce—Religious aspects—Christianity.
    I. Title.
    BV4596.R45S56   1990
    646.7′8—dc20   90-34821

Scripture quotations identified KJV are from the Kings James Version of the Bible.

Scripture quotations identified RSV are taken from the Revised Standard Version of the Bible, copyright 1946, 1952, 1971, and 1973 by the Division of Christian Education of the National Council of Churches of Christ in the United States of America.

Acknowledgments

Special thanks to all my remarried friends who shared their joys and struggles with me over the years. They are special people who have learned to live and grow after great loss.

With deep appreciation to my wife, Carol, who helped type, proof, and critique the manuscript.

Contents

It is far more difficult to create a second marriage than a first marriage when children are involved . . . and it is more important to succeed. The stakes are higher. The risks are greater. And everybody involved knows it.

Judith Wallerstein
Second Chances

Introduction

More than 1,250,000 marriages will terminate in divorce during this calendar year. Statistics abound to verify the escalating divorce rate in our country over the past twenty-five years.

For sixteen years, I have specialized in the area of divorce recovery. Through seminars and personal counsel, I have tried to bring hope and healing to lives that have been crushed and broken through the divorce experience.

Full recovery from a divorce usually takes from two to three years. Learning, processing, and healing do not come overnight. Nor do they come by embracing a quick remarriage to someone who appears as an antidote to a broken spirit.

For many divorced people, remarriage is a viable way of

rebuilding a life. Because a second marriage is far more complex than a first marriage, it takes planning and preparation to make it work. It is to that end that this book is written.

The information in this book comes from my friendships with those who have built successful second marriages. It also comes from those who have lost second marriages. Conversations and surveys have asked the probing questions around which this book is constructed.

Growing in Remarriage addresses three basic topics: preparation for remarriage; living in remarriage; and factors that can cause a second marriage to fail. Each chapter will highlight key principles to be observed, studied, talked through, and worked out.

Remarriage often leads to what our society calls the "blended family." An old movie called it the "yours, mine, and maybe ours" family. The movie was funny, but living in a blended family is hard work. The blending process involves life-styles and histories, faiths and faults, memories good and bad, beginnings and endings, personalities and problems. It involves what was already created in your primary family and what is being created in your secondary or blended family.

Someone has wisely said, "the blended family comes with carrying charges." *Growing in Remarriage* will help you identify the carrying charges and work with them successfully in your new structure. It will take time and patience, often a lost commodity in our society of instancy.

Note: This book may be used by widowed as well as divorced persons.

Growing
in
Remarriage

1
Preparing for Remarriage: An Overview

As a counselor and minister, I have presided over many second-marriage ceremonies. I have watched age-old traditions blend with second-marriage innovations to create a warm and celebrative atmosphere. I have looked into the faces of those standing before me who have known the sorrow and ravages of divorce. I have watched smiles and tears merge as the vows of marriage are shared. The children of both spouses have stood close by, forming an honor guard of hope and love. Family, friends, and well-wishers have affirmed their support of this new union by their attendance.

At times, my own tears have blended with those of the bride and groom as I introduced them to the wedding audience. I too shared their happiness, for often in months past, I had shared their tears of sadness and loss.

More often than not, a nagging question tugs at my consciousness as the couple recess down the aisle to begin a new life together: *Have they done their homework?*

Have the memories been filed? Have the hurts been adequately healed? Have personal responsibilities been accounted for?

The Greatest Threat to a New Marriage

Many people enter a second marriage hoping the new spouse will be able to take care of unresolved business that remains from a first marriage. Heading that list are four needs: emotional, financial, vocational, and relational.

The process of recovering from a divorce teaches you that you are responsible for yourself in every area of life. That is tough to assimilate at first because you may have assigned that responsibility to your partner over the years of your marriage. Instead of assuming that responsibility and figuring out what it entails postdivorce, it is easier to assign it to someone you have chosen to remarry.

A recent counseling appointment in my office verified this reality. The couple had been married for two years after a whirlwind courtship of a few months. The marriage was beginning to unravel because the new husband no longer wanted to assume the responsibility for his wife's divorce recovery. She had made him responsible for both her recovery and her future. His growing resentment toward having to handle her past sent him looking for the marriage exit door.

One of the strongest recommendations I make in post-divorce recovery is to never date a newly divorced person once you are well on the road to your own recovery and growth. The danger is that person will transfer "unfinished business" to you and allow you to rescue him or her. We are all familiar with the classic term *rebound marriage.* Rebounders are simply too lazy to do their own homework. Marriage on the rebound seldom lasts, and you cheat yourself out of your own growth. No one can do for you what you need to do for yourself.

When the Hurts Are Not Healed

Postdivorce, many people have emotional collisions instead of relationships. Emotional collisions happen when you are looking for someone to make your pain and hurt go away. That person can be a quick fix for the headache your divorce caused.

The sympathy and love your parents gave you as a child when you had an injury is easily transferable to adulthood. It is easy to live under the promise that the right person will always make the pain go away. He or she may bring relief but not healing. Healing is often a lonely experience, and it takes time. A supportive and sustaining community will aid in the process, and their love is best expressed by allowing you the freedom of your struggle, not the escape from it.

Can You Afford a Second Marriage?

Finances are a problem in most first marriages. They can be one gigantic problem in second marriages. The unpaid left-overs from the first marriage often put undue stress on a second marriage. Resentments tend to build when prior responsibilities drain present commitments. The tragedy is that this is seldom weighed and talked out before the new love is entrenched. The one uncontested and unchallenged belief that goes from marriage to marriage is, "When you are in love, everything will work out!" A good revision would be, "We are in love and we will have to work very hard to work everything out!" You may believe that love will keep you together while finances are slowly pulling you apart.

Your Vocation Should Not Depend on Who You Remarry

Divorce is often a time for a total reevaluation of every area of your life. One of those key areas is your vocation. Too many formerly married people put off vocational changes until they are remarried. Then that change often becomes an issue rather than a choice. Contemporary society now offers vocational change at any age or station of life with a freedom unexperienced in the past. Since remarriage brings enough changes, it might be wise to plan or think through any vocational changes prior to remarriage. In general, women undergo more vocational changes than men as a result of divorce. Assuming their own economic responsibility usually dictates this. Prolonging that change until remarriage may bring unfinished business into the new relationship.

Remarriage Is Not a Rescue

Loss of a mate through death or divorce usually means the loss of most of your married friends. Married people do not deal well with single-again people. Sudden singleness means rebuilding your support system, for the most part with other single-again people. Tragically, in our society, singleness of any form is more often the brunt of jokes than of understanding or empathy. In many singles groups, the object is to find someone you can eventually marry who will forever place you back in the married community.

Many single-again people have told me they are lost and just want to be married again so they will know who they are. Knowing who you are should not depend upon being married or single. Identity starts with *you*. If you don't know who you are as a single-again person, you may never know who you are as a remarried person.

Unfortunately, there are many people who derive their entire identity from another person. When the other person is removed, the identity is lost. Many married people have absorbed the identity of their mates to the exclusion of forming their own. When the loss of a mate occurs after many years of marriage, the relational props supporting the identity also disappear.

Who Am I Now That I Am Alone?

One of my strongest arguments for giving yourself the gift of two to three years to recover from a divorce is to allow for the healing process to become operative. Along with that healing comes the establishment of who you are at this intersection of life. If you don't know who you are, you won't know where you are going.

Many single-again persons are on a search-and-seizure mission to find the right person who will fill in the blanks in their lives. Those pressures are understandable because they come from human need.

"How can I resolve the issue of lack of finances? Days and nights of loneliness? Poor self-esteem? Lack of parental support in raising my children? Someone to take care of me?"

The answer for many appears to be, "Find the right man or woman and get married." Needless to say, if you presented that kind of shopping list to any potential matrimonial candidates, they would run for their lives.

We still live with the age-old marriage axiom: "Find a good man [woman] who will take care of you." Prior to a first marriage, the shopping list will generally not be too long or the qualifications too extensive. In a second marriage, however, one often operates with the failed expectations from the first marriage list plus all the unrealistic expectations that have been added through life experience. A failed marriage means failed expectations. A remarriage can mean a very long list of unrealistic expectations times two!

I Have to Put Myself Together First

Rejection is one of the primary feelings when a marriage fails. Close to 75 percent of all the people I work with in divorce-recovery seminars have been left for someone or something else in life. The other 25 percent fall into the category of those who left a relationship because they could no longer survive in it. They had been subjected to abuse, perversion, alcoholism, drugs, gambling, and other unacceptable situations.

The feeling of rejection can send you running after someone who will accept you. After massive doses of rejection, acceptance is such a good feeling that it often clouds good judgment. Healthy self-esteem is centered in your acceptance by others and acceptance by yourself. A good self-image helps you operate from the ground of security rather than insecurity. It will take months, even years, to overcome the feelings of rejection and put yourself together in a positive reconstruction. To initiate any relationship before you have put the pieces of your own life back together is dangerous. At times, the desire to be rescued is strong in all of us. When you have put yourself together, you will operate from a place of strength rather than vulnerability.

Some Loose Ends Will Always Be Loose

"It's finally over! My divorce is finalized!"

Over the years, I have listened to that declaration many times. I only wish it were totally true. What it usually means is that the legal work is over, but the emotional work will continue for years to come. And the loose ends will always be there to forever be snagged, snarled, and knotted into a remarriage.

Realism in a second marriage knows and accepts that fact as a given. Even if one chooses not to remarry, the loose ends still float around. The difference is that remarriage often means there are two sets of loose ends waiting to entrap and entangle the new life you are trying to build. It is rather like knowing there are potholes in the road you are driving to work on. If you know they are there, you can slow down, go around them, or at least soften the impact.

The mistake many second-marriage partners make is thinking the loose ends of the former marriage will disappear forever in the excitement and challenge of the new relationship. From my experience, this seldom if ever happens and if it does, it means the new family has moved to Antarctica!

2
Closing Doors

The most important ingredient in preparing for a second marriage is bringing closure to the first marriage. As some wise soul said, "Let go of the past; there's no future in it!"

Because marriage relationships are intricate and involved, there is no quick way to bring closure to them. Divorce is more of a process than an event, and there are many doors to be slowly and quietly closed during the two- to three-year postdivorce growth period. The closure process is similar for widows and widowers. The slight difference is that a divorce can leave you with a mountain of bad memories of the departed spouse while death can leave you with the loss but good memories of the spouse.

In my book *Growing Through Divorce*, the two- to three-year rebuilding time is illustrated by three phases: Shock, Recovery, and Growth. Few doors are closed during the Shock and Recovery stages. Emotional balance has to be restored prior to beginning any closures of the past. The greatest danger to the divorce-recovery process during the times of Shock and Recovery is allowing yourself to be rescued by another person. When any of us hurt, we are highly vulnerable to emotional rescue. Many quick second marriages are simply emotional collisions that can short-circuit any real growth beyond divorce. Many second marriages fail for this reason.

After years of working in the divorce-recovery field, I have found that people recovering from a divorce fall into three groups: the Forever Bitter and Battered; the Quickly Rescued and Remarried; and the Growing and Guarded. Which group do you fall into? The first two groups are self-destructive. The third group is moving toward responsibility. They know the journey from Grief to Growth will take time, planning, and hard work on their part.

Preparation for remarriage starts back in the trenches of divorce country. As you climb out of the trenches, you start closing the doors to yesterday and opening the doors to today and tomorrow.

Accepting Reality

In Margery Williams' book, *The Velveteen Rabbit*, a simple but imposing question is asked of the Skin Horse by the Velveteen Rabbit: "What is Real?"

The Skin Horse answers, "Real isn't how you're made. It's

a thing that happens to you . . . once you are Real, you can't be ugly, except to people who don't understand."

For many people in today's world, marriage is real while divorce is unreal. Divorcing people have to come to grips with the fact that the unreal is happening to them. Unplanned, unwanted, undesired, and unreal! Accepting that reality along with its finality is the first step in bringing closure to a relationship that no longer exists. Because fantasy is more fun than reality, many divorced and widowed people tend to live in their yesterdays and hope they can be recreated in their tomorrows.

Accepting reality starts when we allow ourselves to feel the pain and know that healing is a process that can never be short-circuited. Pain is the process that allows the seeds of healing to take root in our lives.

Frequently, I meet people in counseling who try to postpone or transfer the reality of their loss. In their thinking, a replacement or immediate stand-in will make everything okay again. They will be absolved of the need for struggle, rebuilding, self-examination, and personal growth. That amounts to finding someone else to do your homework for you. The assignment can be completed by another, but you will never benefit by having someone else do for you what you *must* do for yourself.

As I finished a recent divorce-recovery seminar, a young lady walked up to me with a question: "How long after a divorce should you wait until you remarry?"

I asked her to explain her situation. She briefly stated that her divorce would be final in a month and she was planning to marry again within the next four months.

I wondered for a minute where she had been during the seminar when I talked about two to three years before one entered any kind of new relationship. After I again stated that fact to her, she smiled, said, "Maybe that doesn't apply to me," and slowly walked away.

I wondered about her ability to accept reality!

Accepting reality on a very basic level starts in the mind. It is telling yourself that what has happened is *real*. You may not like it, want it, or have any answers to processing it . . . but you have to accept it in order to respond positively to it.

Many people accept reality with a "what if . . ." qualifier tossed in for good luck. From my experience, 99 percent of the "what ifs" never happen. Setting a series of them in front of your realities will only prohibit or delay your growth.

Simply put, reality is what is . . . fantasy is what you wish was but usually isn't! Reality is bringing closure to a relationship that no longer exists.

Letting Go of the Physical

Human warmth, touch, intimacy, and physical presence are gone instantly with the death of a spouse. In a divorce, they can vanish instantly or by degrees. Because of human nature and desire, we have a tendency to deal with this loss by finding another person to fill the void. Every human being lives with the need to love and be loved in return. Hurt and rejection fuel our need for love even more. Many single-again people become emotional sponges in search of saturation.

Often, postdivorce/death relationships that lead to second marriages are founded purely on the physical-emotional level.

Physical need becomes the foundation of another marriage. When the physical relationship weakens, the marriage often collapses and the individuals involved are off in pursuit of someone else to meet their needs.

I have listened to countless single-again people say they just want someone to touch or hold them—nothing more. That is an honest declaration of humanity. The struggle is to stick with the "nothing more."

As they process the loss of the physical presence of a spouse in their lives, many divorced and widowed people become susceptible to brief physical relationships. Too often the brief become permanent and individual growth is again denied.

I believe healthy growth and preparation for eventual re-marriage involves closing some of those physical doors for a time in your life. Because the physical and emotional are closely tied together, relational realities often become blurred. A healthy relationship is built upon mental, social, physical, and spiritual realities. One-dimensional relationships are bound for failure from the start. But once started, they are also harder to end!

Filing the Memories

To live is to make memories. Some are good and some are bad. Both become the collectibles of our life and go into the file drawers of our spirit. Bringing closure to one marriage and an opening to a new one involves putting one's memories in perspective.

Visual memories are usually placed in family albums for all to see at holidays and special times. They are the tangible markings of the days of our lives. Who gets them after a divorce? Where do they go in a second marriage? What do we think, feel, wish when we view them? How do new spouses relate to them? Who is in the gold frame on the mantle? Who is in the bottom of the file drawer in the garage?

Memories live in albums and memories live in our hearts. They don't go away and they cannot be denied. They will continue to inspire both tears and joy. They must find a safe filing place in our lives where they can both rest and periodically be reviewed. Bringing closure to our memories is knowing we lived them and putting them in a safe place.

The difference between a first and second marriage is that there is a recorded history of the first marriage and an undeveloped history of the second marriage. First-marriage memories are often used as second-marriage weapons. It is difficult to share in a memory you have not lived. It is even harder when that memory is used as a yardstick by which to measure you.

A second marriage mandates that you do some homework on your memories. Bad memories of a first marriage should not be your ready reference guide to all that occurs in a second marriage. Quite often, you may have to say to yourself, "That was then, this is now!"

Who Is Responsible for Me?

Soon after the loss of a mate through either divorce or death, you will have to struggle with a basic question upon which your future hinges: Who is responsible for me?

There are three possible answers to this question: my former spouse; my future spouse; or me. How you live and grow will depend on which answer you choose. In my counseling, I find that about 30 percent of all single-again people want their former spouses to be responsible for them in some if not all areas. About 60 percent would like to find someone who will be responsible for them. The smallest percentage take charge of their own lives and do not look for someone else to assume that responsibility. Which one of those categories do you fit into?

Blame seems to conjure up even higher expectancies. Those who blame their former spouse for their present state want them to be responsible for their present and future. That responsibility wish often extends beyond the monetary to the emotional, relational, social, and parental.

Bringing closure to a relationship that no longer exists means closing the door on any responsibility other than that assigned by the legal structure in our society. As I often say in my divorce-recovery workshops, "Always remember, in a divorce, you get custody of yourself." The sooner you assume it, the quicker you will start growing.

The 60 percent group are not looking to pass the baton of responsibility backward but forward to the closest open hand. When all the pressure of living single, being a single parent, and surviving economically and vocationally rain down on your life on the same day, any offer of help from an open hand would seem welcome. But as a friend once said, "Always look at what is attached to the open hand."

Looking for someone to share a heavy load is an understandable desire. Looking for someone to assume responsibility for you is not! It is closely akin to looking for someone to make you happy when, in truth, happiness is an inside job.

Many single-again people set forth with their shopping list in hand, hoping they can find someone who will assume their life agenda for them.

The sad truth is you will probably find someone, but the assuming will be on their terms. Many second marriages end in failure because of misplaced assumptions.

You are responsible for yourself! You may not like it and it may seem like an impossible job that has no end, but the quicker you assume it, the stronger you will become. And the stronger you grow, the less likely you are to pass your baton back or ahead. You will grow to like the feel of it in your hand, knowing you can carry it anywhere without dropping it! You will always face the question, "Can I make it on my own?" Once you decide the answer is yes, you will be very careful when you think of passing your baton of personal responsibility. You will be certain to pass it only to someone as responsible as yourself.

Becoming responsible for yourself means setting some goals for your life that are not contingent on someone else's goals or life-style. It is developing a game plan for yourself that you don't have to give up when you meet a future partner. When you meet the right person, you will find that your game plan and his or hers can be blended, and both of you will be winners.

The two- to three-year minimum between divorce and remarriage gives you time to make some decisions and ask yourself what you want—not what someone else thinks you should have. You have the time to assess where you have been and decide where you want to go. It is time to answer the question, "Can I make it on my own?" and set the plans that will help you answer yes.

Write some of your goals down on paper or put them in your

journal. Set some short-term goals and some long-term goals. Avoid contingency goals. They make you too reliant on other people. Set some stretch goals that force you into new territory and demand work and discipline from you.

An example of a short-term goal would be losing ten pounds in the next thirty to forty-five days. A long-term goal would be going back to school to complete your master's degree over the next two years. A stretch goal is one that forces you out of your personal "comfort zone" and enables you to attempt something that might raise eyebrows. Pursuing skydiving or learning to fly a plane would be challenging stretch goals.

Share your goals with those around you whom you trust. Receive their affirmation as you attain your goals. Affirm them as they attain their goals.

Too many single-again people look to others for their goals and directions. You are responsible for yourself. If you accept that and work on it, you will ultimately look for a responsible person to marry.

You need to be aware that, the more you are responsible for yourself, the harder it will be to find someone who shares your standards. This is especially true of women who have taken charge of their lives. Many men run from women who know what they are doing and where they are going. My advice is to let them run. They are not what you need!

Becoming a Whole Person

Wholeness is a lifetime process. We are all continually working on it. We will never be pronounced whole in this life and stamped with the seal of accomplishment.

31

Wholeness is, in part, our ability to learn from where we have been. In divorce recovery, we tell our people to look back just long enough to learn something from where they have been that will help them get where they are going. Loss of a mate does afford the luxury of a total life review. That takes time, analysis, introspection, and hard work. It does not happen overnight.

Many people enter a second marriage without any attempt at growing in their own wholeness. Consequently, their new marriage is simply a rerun of a prior marriage and ends with the same mournful discovery that they have not grown at all in themselves. Some people even marry the same type of person they were married to before. Personal change and wholeness will not allow you to do that. Lack of it will!

In order to become a more whole person between marriages, a door must be closed on what you were and a new door must be opened on what you would like to become. You have to make some *aha!* discoveries that let you know that you are different now. Some of those moments happen by your own processing; others happen with the help of trusted friends and counselors. Sometimes the discovery question here is, "Who am I now that I am alone?" That answer seldom comes quickly but over many months of probing, searching, and agonizing. Many divorced and widowed people have so absorbed the identity of their mates that they really have no idea who they are on the inside.

When well-meaning friends ask why you are taking so long to remarry, you might answer by telling them you are trying to find out who you are first. Someone has said, "If you don't know who you are, you won't know where you are going." And no sane person wants to be lost on the journey through life.

Even the premature invitation to start dating before self-discovery takes root in your life can short-circuit your personal growth. When you start investing your energies in another person, you automatically decrease the time you spend on self-improvement and your own journey into wholeness. Another person can steal your focus and siphon the attention you need to spend on yourself. That can appear to be more fun, and it certainly can be exciting, but there is usually a price to be paid. Are you worth more than that price?

Healing Takes Time

Wholeness and healing are often a composite package. In order to achieve a certain level of wholeness, the healing of yesterday's wounds must take place. Divorce recovery teaches you that you will carry the scars of divorce and loss of a mate with you the rest of your life. Either the hurts remain open wounds or the scar tissue will form and healing will come. Scar tissue is a badge of growth. It says you have been through the hurt but now have moved on.

Healing takes several forms. Some healing must be done alone, and some in a supportive community of caring friends. Healing involves accepting yourself as you are, forgiving yourself and forgiving others, and asking for forgiveness.

There is no instant healing. It is a process whereby each day adds a little to the desired wholeness. A person must know and experience the healing of the hurts of a lost relationship before a new one can be formed. Otherwise, the new person becomes the recipient of old hurts.

Putting Seals on Closed Doors

Closing doors is acknowledging history, filing memories, processing healing, and moving ahead in personal growth. There is no shortcut to this homework. The ghosts of unfinished business haunt many new marriages and can ultimately destroy them.

Several years ago, a religious denomination attempted to help divorcing people bring closure to their relationships through a divorce ceremony. Some called it the "unmarriage ceremony." It was an honest attempt to help people uncouple. It apparently died for lack of participants. Twenty years of marriage history cannot be filed in a thirty-minute ceremony.

There is a place in the closure process for erecting some kind of growth marker or point of passage. It is a way of saying, "I have been there, passed on, and am not going back." Closure often needs symbols or seals to make it final. Each person needs to decide for himself how he will close and seal the doors to yesterday.

Even the Apostle Paul dealt with closure: ". . . forgetting those things which are behind, and reaching forth unto those things which are before, I press toward the mark . . ." (Philippians 3:13, 14 KJV).

A primary ingredient for growing in remarriage is to close the doors from a previous marriage.

Take a moment to list your still-unclosed doors and write down some ways you can begin to close them. If you are already in a new marriage, ask your spouse if he or she sees any doors you haven't closed on your past. New doors can be opened only when old doors are closed and sealed!

3
Remarriage: The Questions

Over the years, I have listened to many single-again people make statements concerning remarriage. Usually their response is prompted by my question, "How do you feel about remarriage?" The answers range from "Never" to "Maybe someday" to "The first chance I get." In my experience, those in the "Never" group seem to be the first to go while those in the "First chance I get" group are still single ten years later.

Feelings about remarriage usually change radically and often in the postdivorce/death years. Most of our feelings are centered in how we feel about ourselves. Our positive feelings give us a positive feeling about life situations. Our negative feelings bring negative responses. A healthy and growing remarriage will involve two people who feel positive about themselves. If one is positive and one negative, the marriage is not likely to survive.

Feelings and questions concerning remarriage begin to come up after people feel secure within themselves and many of the issues of a prior marriage have been laid to rest.

Will I Ever Remarry?

When you were a teenager and thought of marriage, the question was, "Who will I marry?" When a marriage ends, the "who" is dropped. After you read about the odds, ages, and statistics concerning remarriage, the "will" becomes a larger "WILL." I wish I had an answer for the many people who have asked me that question with tongue in cheek. There are no tests, charts, graphs, or prophecies that can answer the "Will I?" One of the soundest answers I can give is to say if you are *ready* for remarriage, your chances of remarrying are far greater.

If remarriage is a goal for you, work toward that goal as you would any other. Many single-again people are afraid to admit that remarriage is one of their goals. They fear they will scare potential mates away by being honest. If honesty scares people, let them run. They are not good marital material for you!

I am often asked if there should be any preparation in seeking a new mate. My answer is yes, yes, and yes. It should start with the question, "What kind of person would I like to share my life with?" If you have never listed your response to that question on a piece of paper, take a few minutes right now and do it. You may feel silly, and what you write may look even sillier, but it might well be the first time you have seriously put your desires under the microscope. Keep your list, study it, and refine it from time to time as you would any list of goals in your life. You will be amazed at what you will discover. Your "will I" will start to change to a "when I."

A word of caution here: Don't start running all potential candidates you meet in the supermarket or singles group through your grid. As you develop relationships, you will know very quickly whether that person has the things you are looking for in a mate. I realize there are two sides to that coin, but you are responsible only for your side. The other person's list may be different from yours, and the relationship may never grow beyond a burger at McDonald's. Keep your standards high, and don't start revising your list downward to accommodate all candidates.

After making your list, you are ready to cognitively start looking. Where? Here, there, everywhere! That probably sounds as silly to some of you as writing out your qualifications. I am asked constantly where all the good men or good women are hiding. People seem to think they are all neatly filed in some distant city waiting to be discovered. Part of the problem is that people are not honest enough to say they are searching for the right person to spend the rest of their lives with. Looking starts with a decision to keep your eyes and heart open.

After your list is formed and refined and your eyes and heart are open, commit the entire search to God and ask for His leading and guidance. Preparation for remarriage always starts with a direction. It is not waiting for a string of circumstances to march across your life. There are three kinds of people preparing for remarriage: those who watch things happen, those who make things happen, and those who don't know what's happening. Are you doing your homework?

Am I Ready for Remarriage?

Two major issues to be dealt with in preparing for remarriage are trust and fear. One is based on the known of a past experience and the other is based on the unknown of the future. Many marriages end with trust violated. Broken trust takes time to rebuild. If you trusted someone with your life and now that trust is gone, you may find yourself distrusting everyone you meet. Fear will tell you that they may do the same thing your former spouse did. You find yourself searching for guarantees in the trust department, only to realize there are none because people are subject to change.

Trusting others starts with trusting yourself. Trusting yourself starts with becoming responsible for yourself. Self-trust tells you that, when others break trust with you, you can always return to your own secure center. As trust builds in you, you will find it building in others, and fear will begin to dissipate. This is no quick fix that comes between darkness and daybreak in your life. Trust takes time to grow.

At the end of this book is a test to help you decide where you are mentally in preparing for remarriage. It is far from foolproof and is intended only as a guideline and point of reference of your growth and ability to trust. Spend some time on it and think through how you respond.

If you are a single parent, you will have to answer not only the "Am I Ready?" question but also the "Are We Ready?"

question. Children also need to recover from a divorce and do some growing. There are many issues they need to resolve, accept, and experience healing in. If they become part of a new marriage before they are ready, they might well destroy it. I have watched many second marriages come apart because of unresolved issues in the children's lives. I will talk more about this in another chapter.

Are you ready for remarriage? Is your family ready for remarriage? Is your life-style ready for remarriage?

A second marriage is a blending of two different and sometimes very opposite life-styles. I could easily list a hundred different things here that might have to blend with each other. Because we might miss yours, let's take a moment for you to make your own list. If you are about to remarry, your new spouse should make a list also. Compare your lists and talk them through. What can you live with? What can you not live with? I think I can read your mind a little right about here. You are saying, "It doesn't matter. We are in love and love will keep us together." And too many differences will pull you apart!

The longer one is single again, the stronger that life-style becomes. To surrender some of it takes special grace and understanding. As a friend of mine stated, "The first thing I lost was my privacy, and it wasn't even on my endangered list."

There is one other small test for remarriage. Do your best and closest friends and family think you are ready for remarriage? Ask them to tell you why or why not. Don't be defensive. They will always have a different and perhaps even better view of you than you do. Listen and think through what they are telling you. They will often see issues that you tend to either overlook or deny. If they have helped you through the valley of despair, listen to them when you are starting to climb the mountain.

What About Remarriage With Children?

As I stated in the Introduction, someone has wisely stated that "the blended family usually comes with carrying charges." If you have a family that will be blended, you already know that. If you have no family (your own children), you may marry someone who does, and into the blender you will go.

Over the years, I have listened to my many single friends discuss the issue of whether to marry someone with children or someone without children. There is also the question of whether you will have children of your own in the new relationship. There are no easy answers to these questions. Everyone has their own feelings and fears. My counseling experience has taught me that you need to decide where you stand on this issue before you start dating someone. You cannot marry someone you love and spend your marriage resenting his or her children. Stepchildren wars leave bloody casualties.

A friend of mine summed up his feelings by saying, "I have raised my kids. I don't have the energy to raise someone else's kids." For him a second marriage would have to be with someone who either had no children or whose children were grown and out of the nest.

Another friend who has never had children would like to marry someone with whom she could have a child. Since she is in her late thirties, she could well marry someone who already has children and doesn't really want to start a new family.

There are many variations on the remarried with or without children theme. It is not a case of what is right or wrong. It is a case of what you can live with or without. The yours, mine, and ours family is good TV sitcom material we all laugh at. When it is under your roof for the rest of your life, it may not be quite as funny. Preparing for remarriage is knowing what you can and cannot handle as a family.

Should I Marry Someone Younger or Older?

In the single-again community, there is a standard joke about older men dating younger women. The reasons are argued long and loud by both sexes. Over the past few years, any combination of ages between men and women in remarriage seems acceptable. What few people weigh out, however, is the long-term effects of someone older marrying someone younger. At the moment of the marriage, only the present is considered. Little thought is given to the relationship twenty years hence.

In age-gap second marriages, one questions whether love or ego is the key to the relationship. I will never forget one older man pointing his twenty-years-younger wife out to me with the statement, "Look what I caught!" I walked away thinking, *At least she'll have the strength to push your wheelchair!*

Some people in age-gap marriages are looking for financial security while others are looking for a caretaker or someone to take care of. Grown children often have difficulty facing the reality of their parent marrying someone their own age. Dad's new wife or Mom's new husband can remain the brunt of criticism, constant jokes, or failed acceptance.

When her marriage broke up, one age-gap wife told me her husband had done everything she still wanted to do in life and now wanted to be left to his own interests. Both being and displaying an "ornament" spouse can become old very quickly. Once the ego trip ends, often the marriage swiftly follows the same course.

Several years ago, when another friend of mine married a woman his own age, I kidded him about the numerous men who marry younger women. His comment to me was, "I don't want to help anyone else grow up. I want someone who is at the same place in life I am." Eleven years later, their second marriage is doing well.

Do age-gap marriages ever work out? Yes! I have performed weddings for them, watched them, and cheered for them. My observation is that they contain a special set of dynamics that are not for everyone. It is a good question to think about and wrestle through before one begins building new relationships that could eventually lead to remarriage.

What About Pre-Second-Marriage Counseling?

Whether one is sixteen or forty-six-teen, it is still true that dating and relating is all about convincing the other person you are a good person and the best person for him or her.

About 99 percent of the time, the best side of you is the only side that person sees. How do couples get to see and understand the *real* other person?

Generally, we reveal the real person in us when we feel we can trust the other person with that knowledge. We do it by bits and pieces. The more we are accepted, the more we trust further bits and pieces to be revealed. This is no instant process. It can take weeks, months, even years. An environment of trust is built only as we supply the materials.

Time, trust, and testing build solid relationships. The testing part can involve both daily human struggles and wise outside counsel from people who can ask the right questions. Because the people in second marriages come with preformed histories and personalities, it is wise for both partners to take some psychological tests given by competent counselors. In the Resources listed at the end of the book, I recommend several that are effective in revealing and acknowledging the differences in people. They will quickly point out differences and compatibilities that casual conversations over coffee will not. Things once deeply hidden in a person can be gently revealed by testing and evaluated as to their impact on the life of another person. Psychological testing is a must for anyone entering a second marriage!

Many churches have classes for those entering first marriages. They cover the various facets of building a healthy marriage. Few churches have classes for those entering a second marriage. Generally, these couples are left to fend for themselves when, in truth, they need far more help and instruction than those entering first marriages.

Is It Normal Not to Want to Remarry?

This is a book about preparation for remarriage, living in a remarriage, and reasons and causes for second-marriage failure. But it will be read by people who may feel strongly that they are finished with marriage. When others are remarrying and you are not, is it okay?

When speaking and counseling in the single-again community, I have met many people who have totally ruled out the option of remarriage. Their reasons are many, varied, and strongly held. They are not odd, selfish, sociopathic outcasts. They are as normal as those who choose remarriage. They simply choose to remain single.

The most frequently voiced reasons for remaining single are:

1. My children are my priority. I want to give all my energy to them, and I don't want to subject them to a stepparent.
2. I am fearful that a second marriage could also end in divorce.
3. I have been married most of my life and responsible to and for my spouse. Now I want to be responsible only for myself.
4. I want the freedom that comes with being single again.

From First Date to Marriage Date: How Long?

Over the years I have witnessed the "How Long?" answered as anywhere from twenty-four hours to five years. At both ends of the time span, some second marriages have failed while others are going strong.

The majority of people in a relationship headed for the altar want to get there as quickly as possible. Once emotions are fired, time is sacrificed. Unanswered questions and struggles are put on the back burner. A.S.A.P. becomes a consuming goal. I seldom meet people in love who are not in a hurry.

If the scriptural admonition that says "Love is patient" (1 Corinthians 13:4 RSV) is true, then I must ask, "Why the hurry?"

Getting to really know another person takes . . . a lifetime. To not know that person as fully as possible prior to the wedding will eventually short-circuit growth after the wedding. People who marry in a hurry may hurry up the failure of the marriage. Two words can describe the failure of many second marriages: *too soon!*

My recommendation is to wait twelve to eighteen months from first date to marriage date. It is as good a rule of thumb as not stepping in front of moving trains. If you are in a hurry, ask why. If your new love is in a hurry, ask why. Relational growth cannot be hurried. You are preparing for a lifetime, not a tennis game.

The Questions That Remain

You will think of questions our survey respondents did not come up with. They will be valid and important because they are yours. To not treat them seriously and seek the answers will be a great disservice to you.

Some questions are based upon the experience of the first marriage. The most common is, "Am I likely to marry the same kind of person again?" Yes, if you don't do your homework. People who are not willing to learn and grow will continue to make the same mistakes.

Another question I hear is, "Can a second marriage be

better than a first marriage when it was good?" Yes, but second marriages take a lot more work because they involve a blending of families and support systems. People in second marriages must be more open to change. Flexibility must be that family's middle name.

Finally, a question I hear quite often is, "When love dies, can it be reborn in a second marriage?" Based upon what I see in the lives of remarrieds I know, my answer is yes! They all admit it takes time for love to grow again and it is a learning process. Losing someone you have loved and may still love leaves an ache in the heart. People don't replace or remove heartaches. They give birth to a new love, and that love can grow in a second marriage.

Take a moment now and write down your unanswered questions. Then take the time to find the answers.

4
Relationship or Rescue Attempt?

Life would be simple in the single-again world if one could recover from his or her loss, find the right person to share life with, remarry, settle in, and live. No trial-and-error relationships. No rejections. No dating games. No hassles.

Few people are this fortunate. Most reach out and then withdraw, get hurt and rejected, promise to go into hiding but continue to reach out, knowing that growth always involves risk.

Many divorced and widowed people find themselves in a relationship and wonder how they got into it, why they are in it, what is happening while they are in it, and how to get out of it. The two greatest questions about human relationships seem to be how to start one and how to end one.

A relationship can end up as a form of rescue for the persons involved instead of a healthy remarriage. Are you currently caught in a rescue attempt? There are several basic kinds of rescues I observe in people dealing with divorce/death recovery.

Emotional Rescue

Emotional rescue involves one person trying to make another person's pain and hurt go away. Our world abounds with codependent caretakers who descend on hurting people. The more horrible your lost-marriage story is, the quicker they find you. Some come spiritually disguised while others come as parent or social worker types. A few might be well meaning, but others have their own agendas.

A few years ago, I listened to the tragic story of a lady in our singles ministry who fortunately survived an emotional-rescue attempt.

The male rescuer was handsome, charming, friendly, warm, and deeply spiritual. He chose to dispense his gifts in the direction of this very hurting lady. After several months of being charmed and apparently rescued from her hurt, this lady discovered that her "prince" was really after only one thing: her money. She had received a large divorce settlement and had given this emotional rescuer several thousand dollars before she finally understood what he really wanted. He wore his disguise well and probably moved on to another struggling person looking for a caretaker.

In my divorce-recovery workshops, I fear for the emotionally vulnerable as they tell their tragic tales. I can almost see the emotional rescuers lining up behind their chairs. The tragedy is that, when you are emotionally vulnerable, you almost welcome this keeper of hurting souls. A relationship that starts with an offer of help and friendship soon tangles you up in something far more serious. In effect, it is one sick person attaching himself to another sick person, not to heal that person but to force him or her into a dependent relationship.

You may feel you need to be rescued from your pain, hurt, or life situation. Just remember, it won't help you grow and be responsible for yourself. And it could lead to a far more painful relationship than the one just ended.

Relational Rescue

Relational rescue is closely akin to emotional rescue. It puts a person in your life before you are ready for him or her. People who fear loneliness often fall victim to relational rescue. I have listened to them say, "I have always had a man [woman] around and I have to have one now." The "who" is not important. Even someone from Rent-a-Body would do.

The struggle to grow involves confronting yourself without scaffolding relationally. That doesn't mean you don't need people. It means you refuse to use people to rescue you from life's blank spaces.

Relational rescue can also protect you from having to seriously consider the issue of remarriage. Because your rescuer isn't thinking of moving toward remarriage, he becomes a safe person in your life. People in this situation often cohabit and aimlessly go nowhere. Once that relationship pattern is established, it can be repeated many times when one or the other moves on.

The end result of relational-rescue operations is that people become usable and discardable objects. I call them "throwaway relationships." Some argue that these relationships provide "all the comforts of home" without the legal involvements. According to our legal system, that is no longer true. According to our emotional system, we are lying to ourselves.

Financial Rescue

Divorces cost money, and they start a siphoning process that has no end. Single parents know it better than most. They struggle to make ends meet with sporadic child support, several jobs, and reduced living standards. As one single mother told me recently, "I just want to find a loving man with good credit and a regular job." Loosely translated, she said, "I need some financial help."

It is difficult to resist financial aid, even when you know there are strings attached. Some relationships are formed purely for financial reasons. Other needs, attributes, and concerns are overlooked for financial stability. The pressures are understandable, the results questionable. As one wise person said, "Never sacrifice the future on the altar of the immediate."

Some people cohabit only for financial reasons. Some even marry for the same reasons. The age-old line, "They married for the money," is still in use, only finely disguised.

Of all the rescue attempts that come your way, the toughest

one to resist will be the financial one. Try to step back long enough to ask hard questions. Some of those questions for second-marriage counseling are:

1. What is the current indebtedness of both parties?
2. Who will be responsible for what past debts once the marriage is culminated?
3. Should there be a prenuptial agreement?
4. What is the potential or current earning power of both parties?
5. What are the financial responsibilities to either spouse's primary family?
6. When all finances are looked at honestly, is this marriage affordable, or will it lead to further financial woes?
7. Are both parties starting out with a solid credit record, or does one party have good credit while the other has poor or no credit?
8. Is affordable housing available for this new family?

A second marriage is built on a ladder of love, not dollar signs!

Sexual Rescue

There are two questions that face the single-again person in the sexual area. The first is, "Will I ever have sexual relationships now that I am no longer married?" The second is, "Will I practice celibacy during my singleness and have a sexual relationship again only when I remarry?" Relational realities mean the sexual issue has to be answered, even though most people do not put it on their list of questions to be struggled with. It is put on hold until it becomes a sexual opportunity.

The common supposition among single-again people is that since you had a sexual relationship within marriage, you should continue to have whatever meets your needs after you are divorced or widowed. Sex becomes a commodity to be sought after, bargained for, and traded for as well as feared. I have listened to many years' worth of Sexual Singles Olympics Games. Often, I am asked what I think of a situation that has just been shared. The truth is, it doesn't matter what I think—it matters what *you* think and how you live.

I have known many people who decided they would have no sexual involvements while single again, but then become sexually involved before their divorces were even finalized. They expressed a sense of bewilderment that it happened, but often allowed it to continue in different relationships.

Love, intimacy, caring, holding, touching, and sexuality are all intricately wrapped in the same package. It becomes hard to sort out what you are after as you struggle through a lost relationship with a former spouse. When I speak of sexual rescue, I am not speaking about someone who appears at your door wearing his or her "Sexual Rescuer" shirt. It is more your allowing someone to take you where you are not sure you want to go. The danger is, once you have been there, it may no longer be a question for you but an answer. Patterns are formed that lead you to ask, "How did I get here?" A simple answer: You led the rescue party!

Parental Rescue

"Please, somebody, take these kids off my back!" This was a half-serious, half-joking comment overheard as a single mother hauled her three kids off to the car after a church singles event. Assuming the role of a single parent is one of the toughest postdivorce/death responsibilities in the world of the single-again person. After many years of observation, I am convinced that single parents should all receive the highest award for valor on the battlefield of life. The custodial parent often ends up acting as both mother and father to the children. The job is exhausting, emotionally debilitating, and generally thankless. It is little wonder that the worn-out and embattled among single parents cast weary glances over their shoulders for any form of relief.

There is no unending line of surrogate parental candidates, as most single parents will attest. In fact, most people seem to be running away from any kind of challenge in this area. As one divorced man recently told me, "I want to wear a shirt to our singles functions that says, 'Will date woman with no children.' "

Reasons for dodging surrogate parenthood include not wanting the extra responsibility and unwillingness to take on another financial burden. Men and women who have children of their own may find dating other single parents overwhelming.

Parental rescue is more of a problem from the "I need" than the "I volunteer" perspective. Many second marriages become total trade-offs in this area. Too much is sacrificed personally just to have a stepparent assume the child-raising responsibilities.

How do you avoid the parental-rescue mind-set? First, by deciding that you can be the best single parent in history and by learning how to do it. Second, by understanding that probably no one, even in a second marriage, will feel the way you do about your children. You, as their parent, have a stronger commitment to them. A stepparent has only an "inherited" commitment to them. That does not prohibit effective, dedicated, loving stepparenting. It simply means that the birth parent will always feel different from the stepparent. If one knows that ahead of time, it will help build a smoother parenting structure.

In Judith Wallerstein's excellent book *Second Chances*, only a tiny group of children whose parents had remarried felt their stepparents had been more effective and helpful in their lives than the absent parents. The struggle of primary versus stepparent will always be part of a second marriage.

There is no rescue from single parenting. A remarriage will provide help in the parenting area, but it can never remove you from the primary parent role divorce or death placed you in.

Vocational Rescue

Divorce and death are two major crises. They head every list of life stresses. Our struggle is to make some kind of sense out of them and live through and beyond them to new life and growth.

A major crisis always gives a person an opportunity to review his or her own life as well as to set some goals. Often, vocational changes are made at this point of review. New careers are started in new fields. Success often replaces past failures, and new attitudes about personal abilities develop.

Vocationally, people have two basic choices after the loss of a mate. They can continue an established career or begin a new one (or look around for someone to rescue them from having to find a career).

If one has not pursued a vocation over the years, as in the case of many single-again women, it is easier to look for the vocational security a prospective mate might have than to establish oneself in a new career. Because of the economic realities in today's world, I feel strongly that women as well as men need to have careers they can pursue if the need arises.

Dependency Rescue

Dependency in any form is created when another person can do for us what we choose not to do for ourselves. The struggle in a marital relationship is to develop a form of interdependency between two people. Whether single or married, most people live in one of four different modes: dependent, independent, codependent, or interdependent. Take a moment right now and ask yourself where you have lived in your past marriage, where you are living now, and where you would like to live in any future relationship.

There are many other forms of rescue that have not been discussed here. I have tried to highlight the main ones observed in working with people preparing for and living in a second marriage. Rescue is an easy form of dodging the bullet of personal responsibility and growth. Many rescuees will grab any rope tossed in their direction without asking what is attached to the other end. Over the years, I have watched too many rescued people end up back in the sea of singleness. Always take the time to ask hard questions of yourself as you prepare mentally and emotionally for marriage.

5
The Principles of Preparation: A Yardstick

The more one prepares for remarriage, the greater the possibilities of that marriage lasting. The less preparation, the greater the odds that the marriage will fail. No one can know everything, but adequate preparation says you will know more than those who don't prepare.

Preparation needs to be governed by logic, not guided by emotion. Many second marriages happen when two people fall *in* love and fall *out* of reason and logic. I know it is hard to strike a balance once feelings take over. Love is first a feeling, then an experience, then a relationship. The naive person believes two people in love can toss the remarriage preparation and homework aside and all will be well.

The responsible person knows that homework and love go together.

There are a number of principles of preparation that I want to share with you in this chapter. Study them closely and evaluate where you are in regard to each one.

There are four basic areas of preparation: Preparing Me, Preparing You, Preparing Us, and Preparing Our Families. The most important question is, "Are we all ready for remarriage in all four of these areas?" In the next section, I will present some questions, considerations, and ideals for you to sort through. Be objective and give yourself adequate thinking time for each idea.

Preparing Me

Have you been through a divorce-recovery class since your divorce? If you are widowed, have you been through a grief-and-loss workshop? Both of these growth experiences will give you a solid overview of what you are going through along with helpful suggestions on how to survive on a daily basis. Preparation for possible remarriage starts with recovering from your present situation. The antidote for loss is never an instant remarriage. Divorce/death recovery *must* be faced and processed. The recovery process involves pain, gain, and growth. To acknowledge the pain is to open the door to growth. To deny the pain is to prevent growth. Learning from experience is always the first step in preparing you for what is to come.

The second step is allowing healing to take effect in your

life. Healing always takes you ahead, never backward. Healing takes time and doesn't come easily to those who will not acknowledge their hurts and stay locked in bitterness. My friend Dr. Robert Schuller says that one can "stay bitter or get better." You are responsible for your own healing process. Others can and will aid in it, but it must be your own project. Open wounds are never good soil to plant the seeds of a new relationship in. Preparation is asking where you are in your own healing process.

A third step in preparing yourself involves developing a statement of mission and purpose for your life. One of the most helpful guides I have found comes from a book titled *The Seven Habits of Highly Effective People* by Stephen Covey. The author says a mission statement helps you define your purpose and future destiny in life. Goals, dreams, and ideals are a part of putting that together. A mission statement teaches a person to act on life, not live in reaction to life. Divorce is a time of acute reactions. If that pattern is not quickly broken, others will be in charge of your life.

A personal mission statement says, "I know where I am going." It prohibits someone else from setting your course. It is important for you to have a mission statement, and it is important for a future mate to have one. Ultimately there will be a blending of those two statements. A good mission statement says, "I have a direction in my life."

Step four in preparing yourself involves making changes from what you were to what you want to be as a person. A good way to start is to make three lists. The headings are Was, Am, and Want to Become. An example might be:

Was	Am	Want to Become
I overreacted a lot in my first marriage.	I am learning to analyze more and overreact less.	I want to become more active and far less reactive.
I was put down a lot in my first marriage.	I am a worthwhile person with gifts, talents, and abilities.	I want to become more assertive and increase my self-esteem.

This kind of preparation starts inside you. It involves getting in touch with your thinking, feeling, acting person. It is knowing that when you marry again, you will be a far different person from the one you were in your prior marriage. Sometimes working on this with a competent counselor can help. Learning the reasons helps you change the actions and form new ones.

Human tendency is to work on externals and leave the internals "as is." Lasting and significant change, however, always comes from the inside out. Preparing Me is the first step. Allowing lots of time is the key. Only mushrooms grow overnight!

Preparing You

The "you" in this second stage of preparation is the person you will marry. The initial question is, "Is that person *ready* to marry you?" I did not say, "*Will* he or she marry you?" Those two questions are vastly different. I suggest that the *ready* is more important than the *will*.

Let's suppose, for a moment, that you are growing, healthy, healed, and ready to marry the person you have been in a relationship with for a time. What happens if that man or woman is not even close to you in your growth and readiness? What happens if you push him along because of your enthusiasm and desire? If he is not ready and you are, and you remarry, the marriage may never get off the ground. Both parties have to be ready mentally, emotionally, physically, and spiritually for a marriage to begin. You cannot "get" another person ready. Growth is a process, not a push in the right direction.

Has that significant other person in your life done as much homework as you? Is his or her healing complete? Is the debris and destruction of the divorce well behind him, or is he still dragging the excess baggage? Does he spend a lot of time talking to you about his divorce problems? Is he looking to you for rescue? Those and a hundred more questions need to be asked by you and the other person.

Quite often, one person has been divorced for several years while another has been divorced only a few months before remarriage is considered. They try to convince each other that it doesn't matter—but it does. The danger is that one is healed but the other is still healing, and complete healing never takes place because of the demands of the new marriage. That is roughly the equivalent of two people starting a marathon. One starts at the beginning and one starts at the halfway point. It is an unfair race right from the gun.

I have seen many manipulative tugs-of-war among those at different growth stages. I am firmly convinced that many second marriages fail because one person was ready and the other was not. Sometimes the not-ready person tries to convince the ready person that the marriage moment has arrived. Joy and emotion tend to throw a slight haze over rationale. It takes supreme strength to say, "We are not ready for marriage yet." Many people feel if they don't grab the moment, it will never come again. Panic never makes a good foundation!

Preparing Us

When two people do their own separate homework in growth, exam time arrives when they start the Preparing Us stage. There are several "Us" questions that need resolution. The first is, "Can we afford this marriage?" No, I don't mean the actual cost of the wedding. I mean the cost per year for the rest of your life.

I remember kidding a single-again man about remarriage. He dated a lot, and I asked why he had never gotten serious with anyone. "Financially, I can't afford to remarry," he said candidly. His financial responsibility to his primary family was large, his income limited, and his debts many.

I meet many people with similar financial burdens who realistically cannot afford another marriage. They never allow their relationships to go beyond the superficial, thus avoiding the inevitable. Most of them have grown and are healthy and whole. Yet they are wise enough to know that marriage is not a current option for them. To marry again would be to invite financial disaster and eventual hardship into the new marriage.

Unfortunately, some people remarry who cannot afford to in order to have someone assume their financial liabilities. This is one reason for my tongue-in-cheek suggestion to have a premarital credit check run on your "about to be" spouse. In counseling, I have come across numerous financial-disaster cases from failed second marriages. Always remember, what appears on the surface may have short roots. The luxury automobile may be leased, the pleasant home may be rented, and the credit cards may be at their limit. Even the clothes and jewelry may be anchored in the charge-account files of a department store.

In my book *Growing Through Divorce*, I list seven post-remarriage "Us" considerations. Three of the seven deal with money. The most obvious are, "How much income will go out of the new marriage to support the primary family and how long will that go on?" and "Will resentments build to the point of adversely affecting the new marriage?"

The financial Preparing Us list should include what you owe and are committed to pay; what I owe and am committed to pay; what it will cost us to marry, blend our families, and live financially ever after.

Preparing Us involves blending family histories and structures. Are both of you ready for that process? It often involves a mountain of criticism from within and without your family. Not everyone is ready to affirm your new union, least of all, sometimes, your parents. Criticism can wear one or both parties down before and after the wedding.

Preparing Us is dreaming, planning, creating a future together. It is understanding what it will take to make our dreams become reality. It is merging our statements of mission and purpose to give us common goals.

Preparing Us involves the often sticky topic of prenuptial agreements. People ask me if that denotes distrust in the other person. Is it even Christian to consider such an agreement?

My response is that every situation is different. A prenuptial agreement says neither mistrust nor non-Christian to me. It asks what is wisest and kindest and what is really involved financially. Sometimes there are trust funds and inheritances that should be set aside under prenuptial agreements. Financial legalities become highly complex in today's world. A simple planning process often protects future financial disarray.

Preparing Us must take into consideration the role of a former spouse in a new marriage. If you are at continual war with your former spouse, your about-to-be spouse should know about it and how it can affect your new union. Former spouses can easily ruin new relationships by simply wearing down new spouses. The former spouse can be a haunting specter who is always just over the horizon of happiness in your new marriage.

Preparing Our Families

Two individuals can fall in love and remarry while two families simply collide with each other. I cannot overemphasize the need for time and patience in preparing two different family units for a remarriage. Seldom is everyone happy and anxious for the new union. The first line of conflict can come from your own children. The older ones may be especially vocal, and their feelings can run from jealousy to anger and rejection.

When you love someone, you want everyone around you to love that person with the same intensity as you. In remarriage, that is probably wishful thinking. If your children have a good relationship with your former spouse, they may want nothing to do with your future spouse. They will feel no love, allegiance, or desire to have that person in their lives. Their treatment of that person can be cold, hostile, and indifferent.

Family life can become a constant battle zone when children have a poor relationship with a stepparent. I have watched many men and women give up a second marriage because the unaccepting children wear them down. Months of emotional combat can quickly drain your reservoir of love for another person. Adults wear down and out much faster than children.

Some children will never accept a stepparent. No matter what you do, they will choose to live outside of the relationship. Early on, you must decide if *you* can live with that kind of arrangement. Your new spouse will also have to make a decision. Too many people assume that everything will work out down the road.

The major mistake in preparing the family structure for remarriage is lack of time to talk through and walk through the blending process. Here are a few homework assignments to make that process more effective:

1. Spend time alone with each child who will be a part of the new family. Get to know the child, his or her interests, dreams, fears, and goals. Ask lots of questions and listen to the answers. Do things with the child that he enjoys. Find ways to convey your love. Assure him that you are joining his journey through life, not seeking to destroy it. Children, like adults, fear only what they don't understand.

2. Spend time with all the children together. Watch their interaction, similarities, and dissimilarities. Work at conveying equal love to all of them. Work at *not* favoring your own children. Striving for fair and equal treatment does not come easily. Make your own study of each child in order to understand him or her better. You might know your own so well that you will think others' children are just like yours. They are not. They have their own histories, personalities, likes and dislikes. A new family is an integrated, not isolated, system. Everyone has to be included, even the ones who appear only for weekends or vacations.

3. Accept and honor the memories, traditions, and histories of new stepchildren. Everything they are and have attained to this point in time has been without you in their lives. Look at their scrapbooks, photo albums, awards, and memorabilia. Celebrate their traditions with them. If they have had ten years of real Christmas trees and you have had twenty years of plastic, go with the real tree and keep your plastic one in the garage. Loss makes children feel very unimportant. Your acceptance of them will help restore their sense of importance. If they are important to you, you will be important to them.

4. Respect the right of children to have the relationship they choose with their primary parent. Many stepparents allow themselves to be in competition with a primary parent. Be who you are and refuse the comparisons, competitions, and judgments. It takes months and even years to get this area into perspective.

5. Realize that blended families usually come with grandparents attached. Aunts, uncles, cousins, nieces, and nephews are tossed in for additional complexities. When you marry a person, you marry into their family structure. You need to take the time to find out what that structure is like because you will have to live with it for a long time. Even if relatives live on one coast and you on the other, they will be a part of your new lifescape in many ways. They may mean little or nothing to you while they mean everything to your new spouse. It is well worth a few premarriage trips to get to know them. In the second half of this book, I will go into more detail about living within the limbs of your new family's tree!

6. *Understand that extended families need to be prepared for a second marriage.* Everyone has circles of casual, close, and intimate friends they bring into a new marriage. Sometimes those same friends were a part of the infrastructure of a previous marriage.

It will take time for these friends, your new spouse, and you to have a new beginning within that structure. Some will stay, some will disappear, and others will judge. They need time to assimilate the new person in your life into their lives. Remember, a new history has to be formed on the basis of a relational experience.

Family structures are delicate, intricate, and well guarded. Newcomers are seldom received with open arms but rather with skepticism. One has to be absorbed into a new family. It takes time, and some of that time needs to be prior to the second-marriage ceremony, where all the family members stare at one another and wonder who is who and what is what.

Preparing families for remarriage is important to the continuing growth and health of the couple entering remarriage.

Preparing for the Wedding

Prior to any marriage, feelings run the gamut from fear to excitement and joy. As a friend of mine stated, "In a second marriage, the feeling is simply terror!" You can even be fearful and joyful at the same moment. As two people prepare for the actual wedding day, there will be many different feelings and many questions. If the wedding participants are well prepared for the marriage, the planning of the wedding day will be more fun and less fearful.

There are many handbooks and etiquette books that guide couples in planning all the details of a first marriage. There are wedding chapels, bridal shops, wedding rentals, and honeymoon planners who will assist in all the details of a first marriage. There is a giant void, though, when it comes to planning a second wedding. No one seems to know about the rights and wrongs of etiquette in second marriages. I know of no book of second-marriage ceremonies from which you can choose the one you feel most comfortable with.

Many people entering a second marriage want to sneak away to some small wedding chapel on the outskirts of Nome, Alaska, to be married. They almost want to hide both the fact and ceremony from public view. I understand the feeling behind this, but I also know that ceremonies mark our passages through life and they are best enjoyed and most memorable when family and friends are a part of them.

I strongly suggest that a second-marriage wedding celebration be more meaningful than expensive. Things of meaning last a lifetime while the meaning of things quickly passes from the mind.

I encourage people entering second marriages to write some of their ceremony, especially their vows. They need to include their children in parts of the actual ceremony because they are a part of the marriage. When planning for the ceremony, the question that needs to be asked and answered is, "What can we do that will make this event have meaning for us?"

Often, as I perform second-wedding ceremonies, tears come to my eyes. I, like those I marry, know that a difficult and hurting pathway has been walked to reach this special moment in time. Many mountains have been climbed toward this special mountaintop experience. Tears of joy and celebration are a good foundation to build a new life upon.

Marriage etiquette is good for a first marriage. For a second marriage, forget the etiquette and do what will bring meaning, hope, joy, and celebration into your life. At the back of the book, there is a model of a second-marriage ceremony I witnessed recently. It was by far the best and most meaningful I have seen in many years of ministry. You can make your own variations as you wish.

When you are planning the wedding, take time to talk the plans through. Never, never let the presiding minister do what he or she wants with the actual ceremony. You must have strong input into what will make it special for you. Remember, it is *your* ceremony, not the minister's!

Preparing Me, Preparing You, Preparing Us, Preparing Our Families, Preparing for the Wedding—all of this preparation will help remove many of the reasons second marriages fail. You can start today by keeping a notebook of the areas listed above. Don't wait until someone comes along with a notebook all filled up with a game plan for you. Write your own manual for second-marriage preparation. To prepare is to later avoid despair!

6
Living in Remarriage

Today there are millions of people living in second marriages. As we deal with the changing face of the family in our culture, many more will be added to this group in the next ten years. Life issues that are faced in a first marriage are multiplied many times over in a second marriage. As I said in my book *Growing Through Divorce:*

> A remarriage is not simply a union between two people as it might have been the first time. It is also a union between two different families, and if both former spouses have remarried, it could well be a union between four different families. It could double your pleasure and quadruple your frustrations.

Over 60 percent of all second marriages today fail. As previously stated, some fail due to poor or no preparation. Others fail because of the inability to blend all of the ingredients necessary to make a second marriage succeed. In the next chapters, we will try to isolate some of the things that need to be worked on to make a second marriage a joyful reality rather than a sad statistic.

At the outset, let me say that many people leave a first marriage too soon without trying to work out the problems that come along. In a second marriage, people leave the relationship even sooner. When an "I don't have to put up with that" attitude takes over, the marriage quickly dies. It *always* takes two people working on a marriage to make the marriage work. When one heads for the exit, there is little the other can do to stop the retreat.

Before we deal with a long list of realities in a second marriage, I want to present my Seven Keys for Making a Second Marriage Work. They are overarching principles that make the practical things attainable.

Change

Success in any area of life is based upon the ability to accept and process change. The two basic attitudes toward change are reject and accept. People are creatures of habit, and habits, once formed, are hard to change. They even become comfortable after a time. Once the comfort level of a habit is experienced, the need for change seems unimportant.

Often, habits formed in one marriage relationship are simply transferred to the new relationship. Some will be good for the relationship and others will be bad and need to be changed. We often fail to recognize habit patterns that need to be changed until they place us in an area of conflict with another person. Once in the conflict zone, we merely heap blame on the other person and say to ourselves, *If only he [she] would change!*

The couple who sat across from me in my office a while ago were only a few years into a second marriage. Each of them was caught up in unwillingness to make the changes that would smooth the wrinkles out of their troubled marriage. He was caught in his habit patterns and she was caught in hers. Their life-styles were different, their discipline styles for their children were at opposite poles, and both of them seemed to feel justified in continuing without giving way to the changes that would bring them closer to one another. Each pointed to the other and said, "If only you would change!" Fortunately, they are changing and the marriage is growing stronger.

Change is seldom a one-way street. It involves two people sorting and sifting differences and finding a resolution that makes both winners. In order for that to happen, both parties have to be willing to change.

Many men and women marry thinking they will change the other person after the wedding. Most of them quickly learn that it never happens. Some even expect a miracle to effect change in the other person, only to realize that miracles need human cooperation.

When two people remarry, they must say together, "I welcome change and I will change. We will change together." The desire to change comes from the inside out and cannot be mandated by another person.

73

Change is a process that demands a cooperative heart and spirit. A second marriage brings the challenge of change to your life whether you want it or not. It is a lot like razing an old building to make way for a new one to be constructed.

A second marriage cannot be built upon the rubble of a former marriage. A second marriage should bring together two people who have made significant changes of choice in their lives *prior* to the marriage and are committed to any continued changes they must make to build a healthy marriage. To be resistant to the many changes a second marriage demands will doom the marriage from its outset.

Second marriages are places to build new dreams, not enshrine old ones. It takes a spirit of ongoing change to build those dreams!

Forgiveness

If forgiveness helps bring closure to a first marriage, it opens the door to whole living in a second marriage. It is both a relational glue that holds people together and a detergent that gets the dirt removed from daily living. People live in varied stages of forgiveness. To be unforgiving is constrictive to growth and wholeness. To be forgiving is to be set free to love and grow. A forgiving spirit is a healing spirit.

Many people can forgive others but cannot forgive themselves. Some forgive themselves but pile up mountains of unforgiven debts against others. When the "others" are in your daily life, the tension can be insurmountable.

I watch children who cannot forgive their parents for breaking up the family. I watch parents who cannot forgive their children when they choose parental sides. I see spouses who cannot forgive each other for being married to another person prior to their new marriage. I hear hurtful words stack up in second marriages to gigantic proportions.

Real forgiveness means letting go of things that divide people from one another. Barriers are erected when forgiveness is neglected. A healthy second marriage is a place where forgiveness washes relationships clean. It is a daily process and must be taken seriously and practiced constantly.

Compromise

Many of the black-and-white realities of a first marriage turn to assorted shades of gray in a second marriage. Things that were once plain and simple suddenly become complex and intricate. Yeses and nos become maybes. Survival and continuity in a second marriage invoke the fine art of compromise.

In a first marriage, some people always got their own way when important decisions were made. Passive-aggressive relationships are common in many marriages that fail. In a passive-aggressive relationship, there is an indirect expression of anger or a covert way of controlling other people. Feelings are covered up; people get angry and often refuse to acknowledge their anger by becoming silent and unresponsive. This breaks communication and ultimately can break a relationship.

When a second marriage begins to grow, the participants quickly find out that the new relationship is not a rerun of the old one. Where control once was the order of the day, compromise now takes over.

Compromise can involve any and all of the blending ingredients in a second marriage, from financial management to child-raising issues to life-styles and personal habits. Some of the most battle-scarred terrain in a second marriage lies in the area of learning to compromise.

Many women lived submissively in a first marriage and have grown to realize there are healthier ways to go through life. They reject controlling and suppressive relationships. Those who were dominant in a prior marriage must also learn the art of compromise.

Unless there is a warm environment of healthy give-and-take in a new marriage, constant combat will result and the marriage will ultimately be destroyed. This demands a great deal of work, understanding, and adjustment. Everyone lives with their own agendas and desires. A marriage can become a testing ground to see who will gain control of the relationship. When both spouses are strong, the battle for control can rage during the entire marriage. When one is strong and one is weak, the passive-aggressive yo-yo pattern grinds the weaker person into belligerent submission.

The fine art of compromise says that both partners in a marriage will be winners.

Communication

Communication is a key to every successful relationship. Most first marriages are launched with an unending barrage of communication. It starts on the first date and continues through the early years of the marriage. Tragically, it often begins to dry up as the years go by.

There are hundreds of reasons communication is often the first thing to die in a weakening marriage structure. The ones I hear most often are:

1. No one really listens to me when I speak.
2. Everyone seems too busy to listen.
3. Real feelings and real fears are no longer communicated.
4. No time is set apart from the marriage maintenance routine to engage in "heart" talk.
5. Everyone talks all day on the job. They are too tired to talk when they get home.
6. I can never get the important things on my agenda listened to. If they are listened to, they are ignored or dismissed.
7. We talk only when there is a crisis or a problem.
8. No one really cares what I think or feel.
9. I have withdrawn communicatively because I don't want to be hurt anymore.
10. The children get all the attention.

These are the most prominent ones. You can probably add many more to this list.

Those who teach communication skills say that there are five levels to communication. On the lowest level is cliché communication. It is always superficial and, when spoken in the form of a question, really demands no answer: "Hi, how are you? Have a nice day!"

At the second level from the bottom, we simply report facts about others. This is the gossip level for most people. Nothing is given of oneself and nothing is expected in return. It is closely akin to reading the newspaper out loud on a street corner.

The third level from the bottom involves telling ideas and judgments. On this level, there is some communication of your person. Minimal risk of acceptance is involved. The communication is more of a monologue than a dialogue.

The fourth level is the sharing of feelings and emotions. It is the beginning of what I would call "gut" communication. It involves the risk of rejection if the other person cannot hear, absorb, or respond to your feelings. It can also be used against you at a later time. Once you hang your feelings and emotions out on the line, they are there for everyone to see and respond to. It is tough to dodge the communications bullet after you have shared what is really inside of you.

The top level of communication is called peak communication. It is a level where absolute openness and honesty is maintained. All deep and authentic relationships must be based upon this. When it happens, there will be a feeling of mutual empathy and understanding. Everyone will have moments of peak communication in their lives. They are sometimes hard to describe or define, but you always leave them knowing you have experienced them. In a marital relationship, the communications room must be staffed by both spouses. There may not be "more" to be talked about in a second marriage, but what needs to be talked about might be "more involved."

I once read a slogan that probably typifies communication to most of us: "Big people talk about ideas, average people talk about things, and little people talk about other people." A good evaluation of where you are in the area of communication both prior to or living in a second marriage is to ask yourself where you spend your time communicatively.

Some communication flows through life on a daily basis. Other communication must be fenced off and entered into at specific times with no interruptions. The more there is going on around you, the tougher it will be to move into the top levels of communication. Outside distractions will outweigh feelings and emotions, and soon effective communication will dry up, taking the relationship along with it.

Communication is and always will be a basic key to building a growing and healthy relationship in a second marriage and also in life. Poor communication is best summed up in the words of actor Paul Newman in the classic film *Cool Hand Luke:* "What we have here is a failure to communicate!"

Commitment

In the commitment area, I seem to meet three kinds of people: those who make commitments and keep them; those who make commitments and keep changing or revising them; and those who can't and won't make commitments of any kind.

What happens when you are the first type of person and you marry someone from one of the latter two groups? Sooner or later, your spouse will probably drive you crazy! It would be wise to talk through how your prospective partner in remarriage feels about commitments before you say "I do" (which is a giant commitment in itself).

The problem most people have with commitment is they do not think through the cost and duration of a commitment. Because many men and women want acceptance, they jump into commitments they are not ready for as a way of gaining that acceptance.

In a second marriage, commitment begins with the marriage vows and continues when the couple assumes the responsibilities of the new partnership. Those responsibilities are daily and widely varied.

When a second marriage is established, the primary commitment is between the husband and wife. They must be committed to each other and committed to building the marriage. Within the marriage, another important commitment must be made to *all* the children involved. Children from both marriages must be included equally in that commitment. Since divorce is what often breaks the first marriage commitment, the second marriage commitment must be even stronger than the first. If the people making commitments are fragile, the commitment will also be fragile. Strong, growing people can make strong, growing commitments!

Acceptance

In his book *Fully Human, Fully Alive,* author John Powell states that there are five things that make a person fully alive: accepting yourself, being yourself, forgetting yourself in loving, believing in something, and belonging. If you placed those five things alongside Maslow's Hierarchy of needs—physiological, safety and security, belonging and love, self-esteem, and self-actualization—you would have a pretty good picture of the entire span of human needs. We could argue loud and long over which need is most important. They are all important to growth and development. Perhaps acceptance is the cornerstone of the rest. Until we accept ourselves, we cannot accept others. If we cannot accept others, we will live in loneliness and isolation.

Acceptance is the flip side of rejection. Any loss in life is a form of rejection. Eighty percent of the people in my divorce-recovery workshops have been left for another person. When this kind of rejection is experienced, it can be followed by a devastating loss of self-worth and self-love.

Two people entering or living in a remarriage must accept themselves and who they really are before they can accept each other. Once they accept each other, they have to accept and live with their remarriage situation. They must accept living with *all* the people who come with that situation. Finally, once they accept the people in the situation, they have to accept the situations the people create.

This would appear to be a never-ending maze of acceptance, and it sometimes is. In a first marriage, people grow and develop within the marriage. In a second marriage, they often come with fully developed warts, zits, idiosyncracies, and complex personalities. It is easy to accept people like yourself. It is a lot harder to accept people vastly different from yourself. As one religious zinger puts it: "To live above with those we love, that will be glory, but to live below with those we know, well, that's another story!"

Acceptance is a bottom-line, no-qualifications agreement to take another person exactly as he or she is. It does not happen instantly but over a period of time. With acceptance comes a sense of belonging.

When a family structure disintegrates through divorce or

death, its members can feel they do not belong in a "real" family any longer. It is difficult to convince many people that a single-parent family or a stepfamily is a real family. As the family structure in today's society keeps changing, we will repeatedly seek a new definition of the word *family*.

In a recent family-values survey conducted for Massachusetts Mutual Insurance Company, respondents were given several choices for the definition of *family;* three-quarters of them chose "a group who love and care for each other."

Love and care says I belong. I am accepted. I am important. Tragically, in second-marriage families, there are both insiders and outsiders. Generally they are the children. Many grow to adulthood and carry the "outsider" label with them through life. As you look at your "about to be" or "living in it" second-marriage family, ask yourself who feels accepted and who feels rejected and why. Then ask the people who have those feelings why they feel that way. In any family, primary or secondary, it is a tough job to keep everyone feeling accepted and loved *all of the time.*

Lack of acceptance can quickly destroy the harmony and growth of a second family!

I shall never forget the tragic and tearful story of a lady who recently attended one of our workshops. She had been remarried about a year and the second marriage was very shaky. Her husband's family had totally isolated her from any of their functions. They made it very clear that both she and her children were not welcome in their existing structures. Her husband did nothing to change this or even attempt to speak to his family to correct it. He simply left his new wife at home whenever he went to be with his family.

Her question, through tearful eyes and broken spirit, was, "Is that right?" My response was a firm *no*. And the reality was that if it did not change, the marriage would be destroyed through the rejection.

Love

In the closing days of His earthly ministry, Jesus gave a new commandment to His disciples: He told them to love one another (John 13:34). I am sure they were expecting something more profound and that they thought they were already doing what He requested.

Perhaps the simplest definition of the word *love* is, "something you do." You need to do it daily, in big doses, in a second marriage. People in second marriages are living out the cycle of rejection, acceptance, and love. Adults and children are fighting the same battle to be loved and asking the same question: "Will I be loved in this new family?"

The dissolution of family structure destroys the faith people have in loving and being loved in return. A second marriage is an attempt to rebuild that structure and undergird it with a love that has often vanished.

It takes time for love to grow in a new family structure. The ways of love need to be practiced and processed. Some members of a new family reject love for fear of being hurt again by those they thought loved them. They build tall walls to protect themselves. It takes time and trust and heaps of new love to knock down those walls. If love is patient, as the Scriptures tell us in 1 Corinthians 13:4, you must be patient in administering that love.

When love dies, you are hurt. When new love appears, you wonder if it can be trusted this time. To love is to risk not being loved in return. If you take the risks, though, you will learn to grow in love by giving it and receiving it.

In the Apostle Paul's letter to the Corinthians, he stressed the importance of the process of love as an enduring foundation. It has to be given in order to be received.

Loving God teaches us to love one another.

7
Expectations Versus Realities

Expectations are built upon assumptions that are not connected to reality. We have expectations of every person in our lives and every situation that comes up. We are built up or let down by fulfilled or nonfulfilled expectations.

The basic expectation in marriage has always been very simple: Get married and live happily ever after! There probably isn't a person who gets married who doesn't expect to live happily forever. The love that creates the initial happiness between two people is expected to grow as the years go by. People who are in love expect to be happy. When love begins to falter, the happiness begins to disappear and so do the expectations. Disappointment moves in as reality is accepted.

There is nothing wrong with having high expectations.

What is wrong is believing that they come about by some yet-unnamed mystical process. To live happily ever after is to work hard and long at the process. This is as true in a second marriage as in a first marriage.

When a first marriage ends and your expectations about that marriage go down the drain, how do you realistically form solid expectations you can live out in a second marriage?

The first thing to do is articulate your expectations prior to and during your second marriage. Whether great or small, outrageous or feasible, your expectations have to be spoken. The same is true for the expectations of your spouse.

In a second marriage, new expectations are often formed atop the ashes of old ones that were never born or died soon after their birth in a first marriage. It is easy to compile a long list of what did not happen in a prior marriage and expect it to happen overnight in a new marriage. Hope lies in the new person doing what the old person did not do: fulfill your expectations.

One of the saddest stories I ever heard involved the mother of a young son whose former spouse had nothing further to do with the child after the divorce. She began a search for a new father to the child who would be what the first father was not. After several years she married a man who seemed to love and care for the child deeply during their dating days. However, once married, her new spouse clearly told her that she should turn the child over to her mother to be raised so that they could have the freedom of a life the two of them could enjoy without any encumbrances.

Needless to say, this second marriage did not last. Her expectations went unfulfilled.

It is always hard to fill someone else's shoes. If one did well, we expect a successor to do as well. If one did poorly, we want the new person to do better. Comparisons will always be made.

When you live with a person for many years, he or she becomes integrated into your life in numerous ways. A divorce or death does not simply blot them out. Your joys and disappointments with that person will be a part of your new marriage and life for years to come. The mantle of good and bad is usually passed on to the shoulders of the new spouse. With it will come all the lost expectations.

The Danger of Hidden Expectations

Hiding your expectations of another person is a way to avoid disappointment if those expectations are not fulfilled. You can simply tell yourself the person did not know, so he or she is not at fault. However, it will not decrease your personal frustration and disappointment in the person. Hidden expectations can kill the spirits of both people. One doesn't know and can't try; the other knows and is disappointed. Both are lost in the fog of hidden expectations.

Sometimes expectations are not shared for fear the other person will be overwhelmed by them and look for the nearest exit. A marriage built around any kind of fear is endangered. The fear of being truthful can cause both people to go into hiding emotionally. If love engenders happiness, then love also means letting go of fear.

Expectations must come out of hiding if the relationship is to grow. They must be verbalized, talked through, understood, and lived out. The ones that are unrealistic must be junked. The ones that are realistic must be set up as goals for both parties to work toward.

Here are a few hidden expectations of new spouses that have been shared with me over the years. If any of them sound like yours, get them out of hiding:

1. My new spouse will make me far happier than my former spouse did.
2. My new spouse will be totally different from my former spouse.
3. My new spouse will always understand me.
4. My new spouse will have none of the bad habits of my former spouse.
5. My new spouse will be a better parent than my former spouse.
6. My new spouse will never disappoint me.
7. My new spouse will never handle money as poorly as my former spouse.
8. My new spouse will make me a better person and make me happy.
9. My new spouse will make all the pain and hurt from my previous marriage go away.
10. My new spouse is perfect.

If any about-to-be or current second-marriage spouses knew that the above were expectations for them, they would probably leave the country. Many items on that brief list are subliminal with most people. They are what I call "thought expectations"—seldom verbalized but very expected!

I have watched many people go shopping with the above list. It might be fun to speculate with, but it is impossible for another person to live up to.

There are realistic expectations that can be brought out of hiding and shared with a new spouse. Here are a few I have listened to:

1. My new spouse is not responsible for my happiness but will greatly contribute to it.
2. My new spouse will not always understand me because *I* don't always understand me.
3. My new spouse has a character and personality that was formed before I appeared on the scene. I will love and accept him or her as is.
4. My new spouse will have his or her own areas of struggle. I will seek to understand and accept that.
5. My new spouse may well have different styles of child discipline and management from mine. I will not expect my partner to agree with and adapt to my styles but will seek to blend both together for the good of the children.
6. My new spouse will not be the instant relief I need to put my first marriage to rest. He or she can help in my healing but it is not his or her responsibility.
7. My new spouse will not be more perfect than I am.
8. My new spouse will do things that cause disappointment for me. I accept that because we both are human. I will practice forgiveness.
9. I expect my new spouse to love me as much as I love him or her.
10. I expect my new spouse to love my children as much as I love his or her children.

You can continue this list by adding your own honest expectations to it. Remember that your new spouse is not superman or superwoman. He or she cannot leap tall buildings in a single bound, stop a speeding bullet, or be stronger than a locomotive. He or she is God's unique, unrepeatable miracle, gifted with humanity.

Expectations of the Marriage

Expectations start with the person you are married to and then go on to the life you are living out with that person. The two are so closely woven together that it is hard to look at them separately. The marriage is what two persons are building together. It is the one primary thing of which they both have ownership.

The basic expectation of a new marriage is that it will be different from and better than the one that preceded it. That is especially true if the prior marriage ended in a bitter divorce. Too often I hear these sad words after a year or two of a new marriage: "Same old script!" Old patterns from the former marriage begin to reappear and discouragement sets in. At this point, some people choose to leave the relationship while others settle in and serve a sentence called marriage.

What are realistic expectations of a second marriage?

1. You can expect it to be tougher to build than a first marriage.
2. You can expect it to be complicated, exasperating, and tiring.
3. You can expect it to be a slow building process.
4. You can expect some "same old script" times but know that you are writing a new script each day.
5. You can expect to want to run from it every now and then—but you won't.
6. You can expect a lot of outside pressures that are new to you. They come from parents, children, families, jobs, and former spouses.
7. You can expect your second marriage to be successful if you dig in and go for the long haul instead of the overnight wonder.

8. You can expect frequent visits from the ghosts of your previous marriage, but a good blast of reality will make them disappear.
9. You can expect to *not* become a "second-marriage failure" statistic.
10. You can expect not to run when the going gets tough, nor do you intend to serve a sentence called marriage. You can expect to solve the problems that cause the "run or rust" mentality in a second marriage.
11. You can expect this marriage to be different because you have learned many things from the failure of your first marriage.
12. You can expect this marriage to become a "working model" for all to watch and encourage.

Expectations for the Family

Many books have been written about the ins and outs of stepfamilies and stepparenting. Organizations such as the National Stepfamily Association help in the blending and building of a new family. Let's focus on some expectations in this area. Some of the more unrealistic ones are:

1. Blending two families is a snap and just needs sound organization.
2. We will all be one big, happy, contented group.
3. The kids will all love one another at first sight.
4. They will understand new parents, new rules, and new living quarters immediately.
5. They will simply adore and even mildly worship their new stepparent.
6. With a little discipline, they will all act, live, and think like the children in *Sound of Music*.

If you have been living in a blended family for a few months, you have discovered that the above is pure fiction found only in reruns of "The Brady Bunch." What usually happens when families are blended is:

1. You will spend a great deal of time patching the wounds of fragmented family members.
2. You will come to dread that part of the holidays when children pass each other in airports.
3. You will have more spare toys, blankets, towels, and sleeping bags in your home than you know what to do with.
4. Some days, you will wonder what children belong to what parent on what planet.
5. You will quickly tire of being the "bad guy" stepparent.
6. You will want all children to become wards of the court when it comes to dispensing discipline.
7. You will tire of hearing children say, "My real father [mother] said I could do. . . ."
8. You will be loved and unloved in the same minute some days.
9. You will expect God to give all stepparents a castle free of kids in heaven.

If you have spent some time in a blended family, you could probably add another hundred things to the above list. Both lists are shared to help you separate fantasy from reality in the area of expectations. Let me remind you again that some people get lost in their expectations and lose their marriage. Realism says, "This is how things are and this is the structure I have to work and grow in. I accept it and will learn how to do it with the help of God."

I have worked with blended families long enough to see the joy, success, growth, and reward of honest expectations lived out in the world of the blended family. It works if you work at it. You can expect from it what you are willing to put in it.

Expectations in Community

We all have support systems that exist beyond our front doors. They are made up of friends, fellow workers, neighbors, and others. To become single again is to lose part of our support system. To remarry is to rejoin that lost community but with new members.

Remarrieds return to this community with expectations of the married world they slipped out of a few years ago. Some of those expectations include:

1. In my community, things will be again as they once were.
2. We will be accepted as fellow travelers in the still-married groups.
3. Still-married people will understand what we face in a second marriage and a blended family.
4. There will be no prejudice shown toward us from anyone.

The people I know who are in second marriages would laugh out loud at the above expectations. They know they are far from realistic and for the most part, the people they will now best relate to are those who have also remarried and face the same rebuilding struggles. There is still a strand of prejudice in the community toward those in a new marriage. Prejudice comes from fear or lack of understanding. It is more subtle than overt, but it is there.

Honest expectations in community center around knowing you will have to gain acceptance. Some of your support system will be found in those who have had similar experiences. Some of the help you need in rebuilding will come from those who are learning to rebuild also.

Religious community can be especially hard on both the divorced and remarried. In some churches, both groups are treated as outcasts and fail to find inclusion in fellowship structures. Those barriers are generally falling but still exist in many areas and religious denominations. Some clergy will not even perform second marriages unless they are convinced there were legitimate and biblical reasons for the first-marriage divorce.

One of the biggest struggles in community is to gain understanding from those around you regarding the enormous task of building a second marriage. Time, energy, and economics—all a vital part of a second marriage—are seldom totally understood by those in a first marriage. They may deal with only one family circle while you could deal with as many as four, if all former spouses have remarried.

We all have expectations. If I send my envelope back to the Publishers Clearinghouse Sweepstakes, I expect to have the same chance as everyone else to win. I wait for the winning notification. When I don't win, I don't stop living. I get my expectations in line with the odds and enter the world of reality.

Living in remarriage is getting your expectations out in the open. It is having expectations you can plan for and work on. It is knowing that when they are not met, it isn't the end of the world. Are your expectations built upon assumptions or are they connected to reality?

8
When It All Goes Into the Blender

Life-style is a word that almost defies description. It involves hundreds—perhaps thousands—of little things that combine to describe how any one of us lives in today's world. These are the things we have spent years collecting in our lives. They range from which shoe we always put on first to how we brush our teeth, the kinds of foods we eat, and the way we respond to what happens to us.

Our life-style involves attitudes, personalities, mechanics, inherited traits, and a continuing list of daily acquisitions. Each and every one of us is a complex collection of our life experiences. The longer we live, the more we add to that collection. What emerges for public scrutiny is something we loosely call a life-style. It is every one of us relating to life on planet earth in our own special way.

The people whose life-styles most closely resemble our own usually are the ones around whom we build our support systems. Because they are most like us, they make us feel comfortable and safe. It is usually the people most unlike us who make us feel uncertain and insecure. We work hard at building our security system around our life-style.

Merging Life-Styles

When two people with well-developed life-styles choose to enter a second marriage, those two life-styles will either collide or merge. The amount of homework you have done in preparation for the remarriage will quickly determine the nature of that merging. Little or no homework will quickly result in a human collision. Solid homework and preplanning will greatly help the blending process, but it must be worked on daily to be effective.

If two people in a second marriage were previously married for twenty years and are in their early forties, roughly eighty years of life-style are being merged into the new relationship. That does not happen overnight, as most people wish it would or think it could!

The greatest deterrent to the blending of two life-styles is impatience. Not only are two life-styles being blended but two marriage histories are also converging. If those marriage histories are still "current events" and not resting on the "archives of experience" shelf, they will cause chaos in the blending process.

In second marriages, totally compatible life-styles are a rarity. I don't want that to sound discouraging, but let's be realistic: after forty or fifty years of living, it would be a small miracle to find someone who had a life-style that was identical to yours. Even after twenty-five years of living, the chances would be slim. Many people go in quest of a mate with that expectancy only to find out it is not realistic. True compatibility always demands adjustments and the willingness to blend your life-style with that of another person.

A question that can enter into the blending of life-styles is, "Do opposites really attract?" If the answer is yes, then you don't have to worry about blending anything. My honest opinion is that opposites do attract, but for a limited time only. In the beginning, there is excitement and fascination with someone totally different from you. You feel a sparkle in your life that you may have lost. Two things can happen if opposites marry each other: Either they become so alike they lose their own identity, or they are so opposite they destroy each other.

There is always a second marriage of two opposites that seems to work well and defy the odds. I have seen some up close and marvel at their success. I have seen many more that self-destruct.

Enter a Second Marriage With Your Eyes Open

Prior to entering a second marriage, it is wise to observe everything you can about the life-style of your special person. Once you have entered that relationship called second marriage, it will be too late to observe. All you can do then is talk it through and adjust.

One of the most enduring blending problems of a second marriage is the neat person versus the sloppy person. I meet few people who can put up with the opposite extreme in this area. You can be neat and have sloppy children but know they will leave home someday and live forever in their own sloppiness. When you marry someone whose personal habits are different from yours, you can't look forward to their leaving home. They *are* home, and you will have to live with it.

I remember well the couple who discovered after their second marriage that one was a night person and one was a day person. They were so rigid in these patterns after so many years that they seldom saw each other and were constant distractions to each other's accustomed life-styles. The husband rolled out of bed at 5:00 A.M. and was alive and ready to jump into the day. He could not understand why his wife wanted to sleep until eight o'clock every day. At night, he crashed at nine o'clock while his wife banged around the house keeping him awake until one or two in the morning. Neither would repattern, and the marriage finally ended.

A valid question to ask yourself is, "Can I live with this habit or that habit for the next twenty-five years?" Potential areas of conflict cannot be overlooked by telling yourself, "Love will keep us together."

Another common blending problem in a second marriage involves the "do it right now" person versus the "do it sometime" person. Procrastinators drive nonprocrastinators crazy in a short space of time. There are a long list of daily "to dos" in all of our lives. Accomplishing them makes for harmony in a relationship and a sense of personal satisfaction in life. Some people can live a life with loose ends while others cannot. Unless you enjoy being a caretaker and parent person to your "do it sometime" spouse, you will find yourself in the middle of a relationship that is slowly pushing you over the edge. Many difficult habits that people possess do not show up in the dating stage of a relationship. They appear only when the couple is in close quarters after the marriage ceremony.

One of the reasons I earlier recommended some psychological testing was to help you see traits in the other person that can remain hidden until you live together. Tests don't reveal everything, but they will quickly raise some red flags in the areas of personal habits that may be vastly different from yours. People can change if they choose to. Healthy changes need to begin before the fact and not after. Beware of superficial changes and promises that will never be kept.

Distracting Differences

A third blending struggle deals with the highly disciplined and motivated person versus the undisciplined and nonmotivated person. This form of second-marriage union is like teaming a racehorse with a plowhorse. They look good until the race starts. After that, it is no contest. Racehorses eventually go find other racehorses to run with. Plowhorses tend to just plow along by themselves. I know there is an argument for letting both people be who they are. With a few folks, that might work. With the vast majority, it won't. After a divorce, many people get their personal lives moving out of the ruts they once felt trapped in. They will never again be happy in the slow lane of life. If they choose to marry someone in the slow lane, eventually they will feel impeded and end up very frustrated.

In the three blending situations just mentioned, it is not that one person is right and the other wrong. It is a case of them being different and facing the question, "Can we live with that dramatic a difference?" A surface yes is always easy because we all want to believe we can make adjustments and compromises. The truth is that some differences are just too big to overcome and will affect every area of a new marriage. Living with the hope that the other person will adjust to you and make the changes needed is not reality. To be able to blend is to have blendable components from the start. Some things simply don't mix, and it is far better to leave them where they are than to force a blending.

Finances and Possessions

There are several other key blending areas that need to be dealt with prior to and within the second-marriage structure. They are not quite as preformed as the first three and are more susceptible to the blending process.

The first deals with finances and possessions. In a previous chapter, I asked the question, "Can you afford a second marriage financially?" Once you have remarried, it is too late for the question and time for the blending of financial realities. At the extremes of financial blending are the miser and the spendthrift. A second marriage can quickly end in financial disaster unless there is a healthy blending of these two opposites. Most people are somewhere in the middle, trying to save where they can, pay the bills they acquire, and work toward the future. Because a second marriage often involves a monthly financial outlay to a primary family, the first thing you need to examine is how you feel about that on an ongoing basis. If things become tight financially in your marriage, resentment can build toward primary family support. In about 80 percent of all second marriages, the financial responsibilities involve other families. They can become very intricate and cause constant tension. If some of your paycheck goes to support people you are not related to, you may feel some very mixed emotions.

Adjustment in the financial area of a second marriage demands patience, understanding, resourcefulness, and honesty. The greatest stress point is often whose children are financially on the inside and whose are financially on the outside. It is wonderful if everyone eventually remarries and has enough money to go around—but that usually doesn't happen. Some seem to get more and some seem to get less, and all appear frustrated.

Possessions are also blended in a second marriage. Divorce usually leaves a person with one-half of everything. If you spend twenty years filling your house with furniture, accessories, and housewares, a divorce will give you half of it to fill your new house and new marriage with. That doesn't sound too bad if your "about to be" spouse also got half. Two halves make a whole, right? No, they usually make a greatly mismatched mess. What stays? What goes? What is put in the garage? What is added? Those are questions that demand some artful blending. We all have possessions we are attached to. It may not make much sense to someone else, but it does to us. The toughest things to deal with are those with memories attached to them. They are our history. They mark our journey to this point in time. Where do they fit in this new home and new life?

The Need for Understandable Discipline

A blendable discipline structure is a key part of a second marriage. In most primary families, the responsibility of discipline rests on the shoulders of one person. It may be talked over by both parents, but one administers it. The line, "Wait 'til your father gets home!" struck fear into most of our hearts when we were children. It was translated to mean a spanking, a grounding, or some other more severe form of punishment. What happens in a blended family when both parents were the administrators of discipline in the previous marriage—or when neither was? Either everyone gets it or no one gets it. Standards of discipline must be established early in a second marriage when children are living in the home. Children will test quickly to find out where the lines are drawn. They have been known to swiftly destroy second marriages when the standards and agreements of discipline were not established.

Too many stepparents expect discipline for their stepchildren to come from the primary parent who lives elsewhere. Discipline at a distance never works! Leaving discipline of your stepchildren up to your spouse never works either. The statement, "They are your children, you discipline them," does not indicate a blended family. It indicates a divided family and often one parent without either authority or interest. When marriage creates a blended family, it creates new responsibilities that cannot be passed off if the marriage is to work.

Children of remarriage should know *before* a second marriage takes place what the discipline structure will be like, and if not before, then *immediately after*. Even the visiting children who come during the summer should be informed of the system. While there, they are a part of what was there before they arrived.

The fair and equal treatment of children from both previous marriages will take a lot of work. It usually takes six months to a year for a new stepparent to feel comfortable and in charge of new children. It may take the children even longer if they have a primary parent down the street with whom they spend weekends.

Building a Home With Love and Understanding

The blending of *your* children and *my* children when they are going to live in the same home is an art form closely akin to flying a hot-air balloon: what you put into it will determine how long it stays up! Seldom do *yours* and *mine* become a warm and cozy *ours* overnight. Like adults in a second marriage, children come with preformed life-styles and their own collection of baggage. Some have been in search of a new parent figure for a long time and will readily accept the stepparent's children as their brothers and sisters. Others will not, and therein lies the struggle.

From looking over the shoulders of people I know who have healthy second marriages, I am convinced that the two key things for the blending of children into one family are patience and love. Children have to feel the same sense of security and belonging that adults need to feel. It may take longer because they have not developed adult experience and reasoning to help them figure things out. If the new family blending is not good from their perspective, they may hope it will end. If it is good, they may fear it will end and they will lose a family structure again.

Children may well enter this new family structure feeling resentful because what they really wanted was for their mother and father to get back together and restore their original home. The remarriage tells them that it will not happen, and it may bring all their anger and frustration to the surface in the new family.

Early in the second marriage, children in a blended family will alternately hate and love each other. This is an unwanted testing ground they have been thrown into by adult choices, not theirs. They will love the good and hate the bad, sometimes in the same moment. They may decide in the first week of this new family unit that they are outsiders while the other children are insiders. As a parent, you may have to go in search of them and work at bringing them inside this new family structure. Again, allow yourself time. Feelings don't change overnight.

Understanding the children should have started back when you watched how they related in your dating months. If problems were present then and continued to grow, they probably have become even larger in the new family. As an adult, you have to remember that what attracted you to your new spouse was love. What attracted you to your new children was the fact that they came along with the person you loved. This might mean you will have to learn to love the children and they will have to learn to love you. And it all takes time and effort.

No Magic Formulas

Many good books have been written regarding the adjustment of children in a blended family. Some are listed under Resources at the back of this book. There are no simple answers or magic formulas.

In a first marriage, the parents are both on the scene before the children arrive. In a second marriage with children attached, the children are there before the stepparent arrives. There is no bonding that slowly takes place over months and years. It is a spot-welding job at best, and you sincerely hope the weld holds.

In a second marriage, almost everything that preexisted goes into the blender to create a new union. Past, present, and future all become quickly intermixed. Hopefully that process will create a new beginning for parents and children.

9
Adding Branches to the Family Tree

The concentrated blending of two family units is groundwork to building a successful second marriage. Just about the time you sense and feel your new family tree is taking root and growing, you suddenly realize there is a maze of new branches waiting to be grafted to your tree. Leading the column of waving branches are grandparents.

In the postdivorce period, grandparents often find themselves either adrift from their grandchildren or filling a parent role they no longer desire. Their enjoyment of grandparenthood is often marred forever by a divorce experience. Their grandchildren are sometimes moved to distant cities and they are denied the opportunity to be a part of their life and growth.

Sometimes they find themselves acting as peacemakers between grandchildren and their own children.

The Grandparent Dilemma

When a second marriage takes place, new sets of grandparents with no family connections to the primary unit now surface. They often want to assume their new role, much to the chagrin of the primary children. Sometimes the children welcome the new grandparents and the grandparents reject the children. There are about a hundred variations of the "grandparent game."

Acceptance and rejection are two of the most common grandparent games. Having grown up in a stepfamily situation, I experienced these two firsthand. My mother's parents loved, accepted, and cared for me in special ways. My stepfather's parents accepted my stepsister but always kept me at arm's length. As a young child, I never felt that I belonged to them and they to me. I was basically as much of an outsider as my mother was. I wanted to belong to them as well as to my aunts and uncles in that family. It never happened, and I suspect that many other children in stepfamilies know my experience well. It is difficult for a parent to explain the dynamics of what is going on to a child. It takes some years of adulthood to really understand how and why people do certain things.

Earlier in this book, I spoke of acceptance and its importance in our lives. Children living in stepfamilies want and need acceptance by stepgrandparents. Acceptance says, "I belong in this structure that I can hardly understand."

Being an effective stepgrandparent is much like an adoption process. You "acquire" preformed children to whom you have no blood ties, and you are supposed to love them as much as the ones you have known since birth. This is not an easy task, especially if they aren't too likable to begin with. It will take time and hard work. Sometimes love involves accepting the results of another person's choice. Children should never be punished for adult decisions. They need the security of love and acceptance from stepgrandparents.

Guidelines for Grandparents

Stepgrandparents are grafted to new family trees. Stepchildren are also grafted to the trees of stepgrandparents. Both are responsible to make that new connection work. Let me make a few suggestions:

1. If you are a new stepgrandparent, don't expect an overnight miracle of acceptance by new stepgrandchildren. Spend time getting to know them by being with them. Find out about their lives, interests, and histories.

2. Let stepgrandchildren into your life. They need to know all about you as well. Let them know that this is no temporary connection. You want a lifelong friendship with them.

3. If you are a stepparent, make sure you create opportunities for your children and stepchildren to know and be with stepgrandparents. If you are the parent, explain the kind of relationship you would like your parents to have with your stepchildren and vice versa. Don't ignore them because they live in another state.

4. Create situations for family gatherings where all the in-step and non-in-step can be together. Even if the situation feels non-traditional to you, it now exists and will remain this way in your new marriage. There are very few multigenerational family units in existence today that have not been touched somehow by the blended-family structure. As we move into the next decade, this will be even more true. Once-simple family structures will become increasingly more complex.

5. *Allow all the children and stepchildren to spend time with any and all grandparents and stepgrandparents.* Many children grow up without any primary family relatives to interact with. Grandparents add a dimension to the lives of children that no other relatives can add. Real grandparents aren't the kind who come on a card in the mailbox. They are real people who can add a wealth of love to the life of a growing child. Children must be felt, touched, and loved up close.

6. *Don't spend time chasing people who don't want to grow on your tree.* When stepgrandparents don't want to be a part of the new family structure, there will be little you can do after you have extended the invitation. Some grandparents are simply not blendable. Even your own mother or father may fall into that category. You will be sad and it will hurt, but there will be little you can do. You are responsible for yourself, not for them.

What About the Rest of the Secondary Branches?

After grandparents, there is usually an endless column of aunts, uncles, nephews, nieces, assorted cousins, and former in-laws. Where do they all fit in on your new tree? What if they don't?

Looking at all the possibilities of a new family structure would be akin to looking over the crowd at a baseball game and wondering how you could invite some of them to become friends with you. You would have to invest two things: time and initiative. After the initial investment, there would have to be some common ground, feelings, and interests for the friendship to grow.

The same is true of new groups of potential relatives. You have to invest something to receive something. If you reach out, some will reach back. Some will not. Some will form a supportive community around you and welcome you while others will not give you the time of day. Remember, they were there before you arrived. You are the new person. Allow time for the new relationships to build and grow. Much of human closeness comes when people share the same struggles as well as the same joys. That will not happen at a wedding reception!

Families and family structures will always remain a mystery that defies explanation to most of its members. Some are sound and healthy; others are dysfunctional and fractured. Many come with questions that will never be adequately answered. Some people in second marriages inherit family structures that are far superior to the ones in their primary family. Others inherit structures that defy description.

Blend where you can and add those to your new family who are supportive, loving, and caring. Sometimes the numbers will be small but the quality will be high.

Loose Threads and Loose Ends

There will always be some loose threads in a blended-family structure. If you are the kind of person who doesn't live well with loose ends, this will be tough for you, and your marriage will depend on your adjustment to it.

One of the never-ending loose threads is finding that precarious balance between you and your children and your former spouse. A former spouse will always be a former spouse, and that person will always be the other parent to your children. If you can arrive at a place of friendship with that person, the loose ends will not be as frayed. If there is constant conflict, the wearing effect can grind you down emotionally and eventually cause conflict in your new marriage. My advice to formerly married people is make your former spouse a friend as quickly as possible. I know it takes two people wanting the same thing for it to happen. It is really the only way to get out of the combat zone and not allow that kind of disturbance to affect your new relationship.

It is equally important that a new spouse not get caught in conflict with the new mate's former spouse. Feelings can run very high in areas of discipline, fairness, obligation, and finances. There are some first-marriage battles that new spouses should stay out of. There are loose ends they cannot tie up.

Birthdays, holidays, vacations, and special times seldom fall into a livable and agreeable pattern for adults or children of a second marriage. The most ridiculous battles I have witnessed in second marriages often center around special times. The "who gets who for how long" never seems to get in balance. One parent always feels deprived while the children usually have little choice in the matter. They end up being the spoils of the tug-of-war. They can also end up bitter and angry later in life and not relate well to either parent. It takes an immense amount of cooperation to resolve and balance the special-times agenda. It often remains a loose end for years after a second marriage has taken place. Even allowing the child to make the decision does not seem to work best. Each parent simply puts undue pressure on the child or tries to "buy" him or her off.

Making Good Times at Family Times

Family gatherings and who should attend them is another loose end. Calendar holidays and family special times are memory makers for most people. How many Christmas dinners can a family have to accommodate everyone? How many divisions must there be to eliminate any possible conflicts or confrontations? Do some relatives come by your house in the morning, some in the afternoon, and some in the evening? Should you play traffic cop or run away on a cruise at Christmas?

Every blended family must make these decisions. The issues should be talked about and planned well ahead of time to prevent most of the strained feelings and relationships that can result from poor planning. Seldom do I hear that everyone loves everyone else and all can come together whenever for whatever. If a parent has three children and all of them have gone through a divorce and remarried, and the former spouses have all remarried, even minus children and grandparents, you could have a set of relational dynamics that would defy even the laws of gravity. As the family complexities increase, the odds of happy family times decline. As one blended-family mother put it, "My family is one giant cobweb!"

Traditions, Rituals, and Memories

The blended family also becomes an amalgamation of traditions and rituals. Some are retained from a former marriage and some are created within the new marriage. Some are lost altogether because continuing them is too painful. Each new family must decide what is of value to them. Tradition gives us places to tie our lives to. Ritual gives us the security of knowing that everything around us need not be in flux.

A classic illustration of tradition came out recently in counseling with a newly blended family. In one family, the Christmas gifts were always opened on Christmas morning. In the other, they were always opened on Christmas Eve. Because these families were blended by a summer marriage, little thought was given to potential Christmas conflicts over tradition. As December came along, the issue arose and neither family was inclined to budge from their historical precedent. The battle waged right down to the day before Christmas before a compromise was struck. Half of the gifts would be opened on Christmas Eve while the remainder would be opened on Christmas morning.

When a family is blended, everyone should have a say in what should continue and what should be discarded. Simple things like how to decorate the Christmas tree can be areas of contention. Where to go on family vacations can bring joy to half the family and chaos to the other. These loose ends do not get tied together easily.

It is tougher to be alone with your memories than to build new memories with new people. Traditions and rituals mean little unless they are shared. Introducing new traditions can ease the pain of the ones that have been laid to rest. If you are about to enter or are now living in a second marriage, what rituals and traditions do you want to continue and what ones would you like to store in your memory file?

Faith in a Blended Family

A final part of the blending process is faith. What kind of faith do you put into the blender of a second marriage? Initially, one would probably say, "Faith that the marriage works and everyone is happy." No one would disagree with that kind of faith. You had better have it in big doses if you want a second marriage to succeed.

There is a deeper kind of faith, however: spiritual faith. Author John Powell calls it "something to believe in." It gives a person a spiritual center around which life is lived. Some people remarry and allow their personal spiritual faith to fall into the loose-ends category, like some of the other things mentioned in this chapter. You can live with the loose ends of spiritual faith blowing around you, but you will live better with those ends tied to God.

Many people entering a second marriage do not discuss where their personal faith is centered. They may talk about where they go to church or where they will go to church once remarried. Some feel their faith is too personal to talk about.

Faith isn't faith until it is operational, and to be operational, you have to talk about it. Faith says, "This is what I believe, no matter what happens." Faith in God is not based upon conditions. It is based upon God—who He is, what He says, and what He will do. Scriptural promises are the stronghold of faith.

Sometimes a divorce or the death of a mate destroys a person's faith in God. During a time of "single againness," there may be some rebuilding of faith in God while trying to make sense of life's situations. This may also be a time of depressed faith.

Preparing for and living in a second marriage demands a faith review for those involved. If faith in God has been shaken, is it now restored? Are the two people in this second marriage in a place where their faith can be shared and both will be strengthened? Is their faith in God strong enough to support the foundation upon which this new relationship will be built?

The Roots of Faith

A second marriage involves your faith and your spouse's faith coming together. Faith always takes root when people make decisions to follow God. Some who have never made that kind of decision make it during a crisis such as divorce or death. Others make it when they see it working in the life of someone they respect or love. If there was little or no faith in God in a first marriage, those embarking on a second marriage want to be sure that this marriage will help set their new faith in God in motion.

Since people don't always marry inside their particular religious community, another question has to be talked through: "What kind of religious community will we belong to once remarried?" If one has spent a lifetime in the Presbyterian church, it can be difficult to leave that and become a Baptist or Lutheran. Whose roots do you keep? Whose do you cut? Should you belong to both? Should you find something new?

A blended marriage is a blending of faith structures. The true center is a faith in God, but a life of faith can be lived out in many different faith communities. It is seldom a case of the right one versus the wrong one but a place where both can grow spiritually and be nourished by a supportive community.

The Unlisted Blendables

In this chapter, I have listed some common second-marriage ingredients that will go into the blending process. There are many more of equal importance. Each day of a second marriage, issues will be raised that were not present the day before. The key to building a healthy second marriage is to deal with situations and not deny their existence. It is easy to wish life were simpler, but wishing won't make it so.

There will be few easy answers and fewer instant answers. Much of the work in building a second marriage is "process" work. If you understand that going into the marriage, it will make the adjustments easier. As one friend stated, "The equation for a second marriage is one plus one times four!" I think what he really said was that second marriages are four times harder than first marriages.

A second marriage is a blending of many people with many different histories. New situations will test and try those people and affect the life they are building together. They will need the help of one another every day, along with the help of God.

10
The Seasons of Remarriage

As I mentioned in my book *Growing Through Divorce*, the two-to three-year recovery from a divorce experience is illustrated by three stages: Shock, Recovery, and Growth. The amount of time spent in each stage is relative to the individual and what was experienced in the divorce. These stages help mark the progress of growth and the rebuilding of a life.

Most of our journey through life is marked by stages. We may not like the ones we have to pass through to get to better places, but we seldom can avoid the struggles if we want to really grow. The greatest problem divorced people face is wanting to short-circuit their growth by remarrying before they are ready. One of the greatest gifts in divorce recovery is the gift of time. Time brings healing and a better perspective of growth opportunities.

As there are stages of growth in divorce recovery, there are stages of growth in the overall process of blending your life and family with the life and family of another person. Since we all need yardsticks by which to measure our growth, I want to share several you can use in the remarriage process. Let's call them the Seasons of Remarriage: Spring, Summer, Fall, and Winter.

Spring

In nature, Spring typifies new life, new beginnings, a fresh start. It signifies the closing of a dull, drab, cold time of the year. There is more excitement and preparation for Spring than perhaps any other time of the year. It says loudly, "Happy days are here again!"

The Seasons of Remarriage start with the building of a relationship that will eventually move to the altar of marriage. The formation and growth of that relationship will have all the excitement and newness that springtime has on anyone's calendar.

Spring can have reminiscent tones of another era called adolescence. All the feelings and fears have returned, only you are twenty years older. Excitement and panic constantly change places on your emotional thermometer.

The Spring of Remarriage is when all the planting, nurturing, and preparing for the future is born. It is when the risks are taken and the trust assured. It is when the soil of life is stirred with the confidence of a gardener who has done his or her homework. Questions and uncertainties abound as a new relationship takes root. The fear of a new rejection sometimes lingers around the edges of this new season in your life. Haunting questions are put to rest only as the relationship matures and grows.

Spring is when the questions are asked, the fears confessed, the mistakes owned, the plans and dreams shared. It is a time to go slowly. Growth in Spring cannot be hurried. The relationship must be nurtured. The future of a healthy, successful remarriage rests on the care it receives while it is being formed.

A healthy time span from the first date to the moment of remarriage is a year to eighteen months. That may sound like one very long Spring compared to the few short months on the annual calendar. Many people feel if they don't quickly marry once the relationship is under way, it will fizzle. If that is all the strength is has, let it fizzle. If it is real, it will last and grow stronger, not weaker. There are few good arguments to hurry a relationship into maturity. Those who try to push the relationship only tend to weaken it.

The Spring of Remarriage is a time to enjoy. It can be filled with a sense of romance long lost or never experienced in a first marriage. It brings with it a sense of vitality and adventure. A new person is now a growing part of your life. You are making a new beginning with that person.

Preparation for remarriage is planting the right things in your life and allowing those things time to grow to maturity. When they have grown, it is time to enjoy that growth. In the context of spring, it would be smelling the flowers and enjoying them.

In the Seasons of Remarriage, Spring is when a new relationship is formed and that relationship is ultimately finalized by marriage.

Summer

The Summer of Remarriage usually covers the first year of that new union. It is a time when the joys and excitements should outweigh the problems, if you have done your homework. If not, you may have a lot of thunderstorms in your first Summer. Summer in remarriage is normally a honeymoon time. It is sharing, discovering, adjusting, planning, and enjoying a new relationship. The focus of the love of two people for each other is at the center, and any existing problems are way out on the edges.

There is an excitement about meeting and knowing all the new people who are already a part of your new spouse's life. Going new places, doing new things, and sharing ups and downs keep the experience new. Even the adventure of becoming a stepparent is exciting. Planning for the birth of any children created in this new union makes life itself fresh and vital.

When you are enjoying it, the Summer of Remarriage can never last long enough. Optimism is the rule of the day in this new relationship. You are a team again—a *you and me* against the world! No more singles meetings. No more dating disappointments. No more playing relational games. You have found a partner to play the game of life with. The Summer of Remarriage loudly says you are not alone anymore.

In the first year of a new marriage, most of the people I

have performed ceremonies for live just an inch or two away from euphoria. The ones who never thought they would re-marry are even closer to that state. Some even become sales-men for remarriage! The Summer of Remarriage is happiness reclaimed for many single-again people who thought happi-ness in married form was forever lost.

Fall

The Fall of Remarriage is similar to harvesttime. In nature, it is the result of the planting, watering, growing, and coming of age. In remarriage, it usually appears between years two and five. It happens when you realize that continued love and consistency produce results. There is a maturity settling in that lets you know you did not marry into a perfect situation, but the imperfect is workable and it will not defeat you.

Sadly, many second marriages fall apart between two and five years. Spouses begin to take each other for granted. They don't work on their marriage relationship or the relationships around them in the family. Much of the dazzle and glow disappears from what once was new. Comparisons are made to one's first marriage.

Between years two and five, the marriage either matures or goes sour. Here are some suggestions to help you through this potentially difficult time:

1. *Let reality take over from fantasy.* Fantasy says you can live with your head in the clouds forever. Reality says you have to pay the bills, discipline the kids, mow the lawn, fix the car, chase a few of yesterday's ghosts away, take aspirin, and re-alize there are no perfect people living in second marriages.

2. *Realize there are as many myths in second marriages as first marriages.* Trade in any myths you might have for large doses of reality. Understand and know that stable people can't anchor their lives to myths.

3. *Watch out for the ruts!* The same ones that sidetracked a first marriage can cause problems in a second marriage. Many people repeat patterns because they are most familiar with them.

4. *Do frequent marriage reviews.* Ask the hard questions. Review the problem areas. Update your plans and goals. Get input from everyone involved in the new family structure.

5. *Stop looking for exits and start looking for entrances!* Don't take the easy way out if the marriage isn't what you expected. Get to work and make it what you would like it to be.

The Fall of Remarriage is a time for letting the marriage come to maturity. It will demand care and tending if it is to produce good fruit.

Winter

On the surface, the Winter of Remarriage probably sounds like a period of deep freeze before one mate or the other dies. In nature, winter means a time of rest in preparation for renewal. In remarriage, it means that space of time beyond the fifth or sixth year, when you know you have built a solid foundation in this new relationship and the marriage can rest on that foundation and never be dislodged. Realities have been accepted, solutions to problems have been found, adjustments have been made, love has grown. The word *remar-*

ried becomes obsolete, and you begin to feel as if you have always been in this current marriage.

Thoughts of your first marriage are so distant, you have to work to remember them. You have forgotten how to spell the word *divorce*. Stepfamilies seem normal to you. There is a sense of security, familiarity, and well-being as life flows around you.

Couples I married ten or more years ago now seem to me to have been married to each other forever. I seldom think of them as being in second marriages. They seldom think of themselves as being in second marriages. All admit to having worked hard at building their marriages. Most could write their own books on their journeys and offer sound advice. Many have been a part of this book by responding to surveys. I have watched them grow as individuals and as couples. I have watched their children and stepchildren grow and build their own lives. I have witnessed the love and admiration they have for one another as extended family members. They have made the journey from Spring to Winter. They have refused to become statistics and fatalities in the land of remarriage. They are the reason I believe in remarriage!

11
Second Marriages in Trouble

In the last part of this book, we want to talk about the reasons second marriages fail. Fifty percent of all first marriages end in divorce. As high as 65 percent of second marriages fail. There are always warning signs that precede the termination of a marriage. Some are barely discernible while others advertise themselves loudly. Too often, no one is listening or watching the warning signs as they appear.

Some years ago, in her book, *The American Way of Divorce*, Dr. Sheila Kessler published a Divorce Time Line to illustrate how marriages end and how people process their divorces. It is applicable to second as well as first marriages.

The first stage of decline in a marriage is when *disappoint-*

ments are experienced and little or nothing is done by either party to resolve them.

Unresolved disappointments produce a second stage of marital decline: *erosion*. Very few marriages die overnight. Most erode over a period of time. Much like the process of erosion in nature, little attention is given to what is happening until something or someone is dramatically affected.

When human relationships begin to erode, a third dynamic takes place: *detachment*. As a relationship declines, people begin to distance themselves from each other. The first places they unhook are mentally, emotionally, and communicatively. Physically, they can still be married, have a sexual relationship, and even keep doing their "marriage maintenance work." As the distance between them increases, however, the marital relationship disintegrates. It is at this juncture that one spouse or the other (or maybe both) may become involved with another person. When a person is vulnerable and drifting, there will always be someone around the next corner ready to fill the void. Few third-party relationships—affairs— are planned. Most just happen when a marriage is weakening. Once they happen, the result is usually the fourth stage: *separation*. Simply defined, one partner moves out of the house and the physical tie is broken.

Separation is often the beginning of a divorce experience. Few people separate in order to work at putting their marriage back together. *Separation* may sound better than *divorce*, but usually it is the first step of a process that will ultimately end the marriage.

After separation, a fifth stage called *mourning* begins. This is the beginning of a period of grief connected to the loss of a relationship. Any type of loss is generally accompanied by mourning. It takes many forms and can last for many months. It contains the ingredients of anger, guilt, rejection, loss of self-esteem, and many others. Mourning is the recognition that a marriage has died.

After some months, a sixth stage called *second adolescence* is entered. It is a time for regrouping and new beginnings and often closely parallels one's first adolescence. The basic difference is that you are much older and you may have lost some of your "bouncability." After six months to a year, the final stage kicks into gear: *good growth*. This happens when you assume responsibility for yourself and take control of your life. It can involve social readjustment, pain, independence, and relief.

When I teach this Divorce Time Line in workshops, many people tell me they wish they had known about it when their marriages were getting shaky. If your first marriage ended in divorce, it would be a good idea to stop here, go back, and trace it through the time line. If you are entering a second marriage, keep the time line around as a measuring stick. If you are already remarried, take a quick measurement of your marriage stability right now.

Most people get so busy with living that they tend to take things for granted. When you start taking your marriage for granted, someone else may steal it from you!

Many second marriages end because the people in them have never taken the time to assess why their first marriages failed. Most seem to be content with saying it was "her fault" or "his fault" or a third party's fault. Passing the blame is a game we all learned well in childhood. Once perfected, it can become a lifetime preoccupation. Why did *your* first marriage end? What have you learned from it that you can utilize to make your second marriage better? Are you transferring baggage from your first marriage to your second?

Causes for the failure of a first marriage can be the same for a second marriage. I know this from counseling couples in troubled second marriages. They shake their heads and ask, "Why?" Most of them already know the answer. They were unwilling to take the time to sort, sift, work, and grow themselves. They were too willing to hand the keys to their healing to someone else.

There are many reasons for the failure of first and second marriages. Let me list the ones I have compiled from working in the divorce-recovery field.

The Use-and-Discard Mentality

People are slowly becoming "throwaways" in our society. Their value to other humans is declining. We use people for our own ends and then discard them. Many marriages are ending today after twenty-five to forty years of union. People are walking away from them with little regard for the emotions, needs, or feelings of their spouses. They remarry and move away, and little is said or even thought about the discarded person.

In my divorce-recovery seminars, there are two kinds of people: those who were left for another person and those who chose to leave something they could no longer live with. About 75 percent of my audiences are comprised of the first group. The other 25 percent involve those who left alcoholics, homosexuals, deviants, and so on. Often, the "for better or worse" is replaced by "until the going gets tough . . . then I'm gone." It is little wonder that so many divorcing people from long-term marriages have lost most of their self-worth. The throwaway mentality is the ultimate form of rejection. We seem to have forgotten the credo, "Things are to use, people are to love."

The Microwave Mentality

If you have a problem, you can find an instant answer. Our society advertises this kind of thinking in every area of life. It is almost as if you should not have a problem, but if you do, you can quickly fix it with the right cure.

There are problems in marriage because there are people in marriage and people have problems. Problems are a part of living, and it takes time to find answers to them. Since we have become trained to the "quick fix" mind-set, when we can't solve something instantly, we want to walk away from it. When problems surface in a marital relationship, it seems easier to walk away from them than to work long and hard to solve them. Many people simply go in search of someone who doesn't have the problems they find themselves mired in.

Even people who go to professional counselors tend to want solutions to their struggles in two or three sessions. The thought of a year of counseling sends a person back to the microwave mentality. Many marriages that dissolve could be saved if only the participants would avoid the quick-fix mentality. When problems are not resolved in a first marriage, they will often be transferred to the second marriage. If unresolved there, they might be passed on to a third marriage. There are no free lunches and no quick fixes!

The Two-Career Mentality

As we move into the nineties, husband-and-wife teams will deal more acutely with the economic reality of a two-career household. That kind of existence will put increasing pressure on any marriage. When both people work long hours, they will have little energy emotionally and physically to give to their family or to each other. Since more time will be spent in the workplace, much of their lives will revolve around their jobs. Home will become a place to sleep, wash the car, pay the baby-sitter, and visit on weekends. Add weekend church and community activities to that agenda, and you have a tired group chasing after each other fifty weeks of the year. (The other two weeks are for vacation!)

Too much pressure creates tired people. Tired people live in tired marriages. Tired marriages are vulnerable to breakdowns.

The Meism Mentality

Culturally, the seventies were known as the "me decade." The slogan of the times was, "If it feels good, do it!" It really didn't matter how the "it" made anyone else feel. The "me" deserved the "it". In the early eighties, some of the "me" faded, only to reappear in the late eighties. As we move into a new decade, the "me" issue is soundly affecting the breakup of many marriages. It is a form of egotism that says, "I can have what I want. If I cannot have it in this marriage, I will look elsewhere for it." A healthy marriage is not a place of independence but interdependence. It is not a place of "me"; it is a place of "us."

The Frontier-Marriage Mentality

From the early days of marriage in our country, a man would set out to find a "good woman" who could cook, sew, keep house, and raise children. A woman would set out to find a "good man" who would support her family, work steadily, and keep a roof over her head. It probably worked well on the frontier, but its outcome caused many married people to live in a state of dependence. If one did not fulfill his or her requirements, the marriage often suffered.

We are no longer on the frontier, but men and women (even the kind about to remarry) still search for the same basic things our frontier forefathers looked for in each other.

The reality of living in this end of the twentieth century would tell us that interdependency is a healthier way to live in marriage than dependency. This means that roles once assigned to men and women have changed. Frontier-marriage mentality seldom works in modern-day America. Marriage today is a shared relationship with equally shared and sometimes switched responsibilities. It has little to do with "macho" or women's liberation. It has everything to do with sharing in the growth of a marriage and fulfilling its responsibilities.

Interdependent living cannot succeed with a "women do this" and "men do that" mentality. In a marriage, tasks must be equally shared and roles must often merge.

The Mobile Mentality

The average American family moves once every three to five years. The remarried or blended family may move even more often. Most people move for vocational reasons, such as a promotion or job change. Little thought is given to quality of life, support systems, or family disruption when a vocational move becomes imminent. This kind of mobility leaves both adults and children without roots or a sense of belonging in one place.

It takes a long time to make a new community home. Just about the time it begins to feel like home, another move may cut the cords and drop you into a strange new world.

Divorce often sets new moves in motion for entire families. Not only is the family unit broken up, but it also may be separated permanently by thousands of miles. Children are usually more affected by moves than adults. A child can become totally withdrawn and highly dysfunctional when forced into continual moves.

When a stepfamily is formed by remarriage, that union may be precipitated by another move of many miles. Children can quickly develop deep resentments toward stepparents who they feel have forced them to move. Since most children have little input into projected family moves, they often feel a sense of powerlessness over their lives. Hostilities surface and discipline and control become giant problems for the new parents.

Frequent moves can contribute to divorces in second as well as first marriages. It is not the physical move as much as the disruption to all involved. Stability and routine are great contributing factors to a normal existence. When they are removed, life can be plagued by too many loose ends.

Lack of Premarriage Training

Realistically, the failure rate of second marriages should be minimal. The one thing a formerly married person can take into a second marriage is experience. You cannot take that into a first marriage. Even if you read books and go to pre-marital classes, you still will not have married-life experience. In my divorce-recovery seminars, I often ask the question, "What did you know about marriage before you got married?" The answer is always, "Nothing."

Preparation and experience always go hand in hand. You can prepare for an experience and the experience will validate your preparation. Generally, there is little preparation for a first marriage. In a second marriage, too many people rely on their past experience and do minimal or no preparation. The first part of this book addressed the issue of preparation.

Preparation in a first marriage involves two people. In a second marriage, it can involve an entire crowd. My rule is the more people involved, the more preparation needed and the more time required for that preparation.

Poor Communication

Earlier in this book, I spoke about the levels of commu-nication and the need for good communication. When a marriage begins to break down, communication is usually the first thing to go. Words may still be spoken, arguments may be on the daily menu, but effective communication will be absent. A successful marriage cannot survive on marriage-maintenance talk. There has to be a place where heart sounds are given and received. Heart sounds communicate one's thinking, feeling, acting self. The tough part about this kind of communication is that there has to be a recipient. Heart sounds cannot be left hanging in the air. They must be absorbed by another caring heart.

In a second marriage, effective communication begins with the husband and wife and must include all the members of the immediate family structure. All the lines must be kept open for the new relationships to form and grow. Poor communication between spouses will hasten the breakdown of a first marriage. Poor communication between everyone in a blended family will bring the same results. To have a growing sense of belonging and identity, people have to be seen and heard. To be heard means someone has to be listening. To be a listener is to be a good communicator!

Mid-Life Crisis

It is debated, discussed, and denied but it doesn't go away. You can call it by other names, but the end results are the same. It is mystical, unpredictable, and defies logical explanation. It is commonly called a mid-life crisis. It ends many first marriages and starts second marriages. It is constantly analyzed and researched by counselors and therapists. Those who have gone through a mid-life-crisis divorce keep trying to find out why.

Over the years, I have witnessed firsthand the hundreds of variations of mid-life divorces. I still have more questions than logical answers. I see the lives wrecked by mid-life divorce. I watch the growing disdain and separation between children and parents who go through this experience. It creates two areas of devastation in people's lives: It destroys the primary family and can quickly destroy the secondary family because the second marriage is often built on the debris of the first marriage. Mid-life-crisis remarriages are often rebound marriages that happen only days after the divorce is finalized. Little if any consideration is given to anything, including primary children.

Recently, I was astounded as the fifty-year-old father who was involved in an affair told me very matter-of-factly that everyone in his primary family would do just fine if he ended his thirty-year marriage and married the person he was now involved with. He seemed to feel no guilt for what he was doing and treated every issue I brought up with a disdainful lack of concern for anyone's feelings but his own. I wanted to send him to visit two other men I knew who had done what he was about to do and had ruined their own lives as well as the lives of others as a result.

Mid-life-crisis remarriages leave many people in a state of shock, searching for some realistic explanation. Seldom does one appear that makes any sense. My feeling is that 40 to 50 percent of all divorces and remarriages today are the direct result of some form of mid-life crisis. The ages of the adults involved run from forty to sixty.

There are predictable crises in living that consume all of us at one time or another. The secret to surviving a crisis is to get some help in processing it and learn to wait for it to pass. It may be precipitated by biological or emotional changes. A mentality that says throw away what you have and get something brand-new will not solve the crisis. It will only prolong it and endanger more people.

A mid-life crisis is not something to joke about. It is a form of change and struggle that often blindsides a person. During the crisis, sound judgment goes out the window and life is lived for the moment. Rash decisions are made that can affect the rest of one's life as well as the lives of others. When you think about remarriage, make sure it will not be built upon the shaky foundation of the other person's mid-life divorce.

Mid-life crises happen to both men and women. My observation is that men remarry more quickly when going through mid-life crises. Women tend to move more toward careers or single living as a result of their crises. The need in both to either give up or change their lifelong responsibilities is apparent. As pressures mount up in the next decade, mid-life divorces and remarriages will also increase. Both will leave many people asking why.

Many of the reasons listed for a first divorce will become the seedbed for the failure of a second marriage. We can learn from reasons and measure from checklists, but they are valid only if we can incorporate their teachings into our lives. Perhaps the reasons you have come up with for your failed marriage are not on this list. One I listen to often is, "I married the wrong person in the first place." That may be a valid reason for many and is undoubtedly true. Some admit to knowing the marriage was wrong after only a few months, and finally, after twenty or thirty years of misery, the marriage was brought to closure.

Another statement I hear is, "I married for the wrong reasons." Young people often marry in their teens simply to get away from their parents. Still others marry people with money because they have none. You can remarry someone after a divorce just so you will not grow old by yourself or run out of money. The "wrong reason" marriage seldom works in primary or secondary form.

Wrong person and wrong reason can cause marital failure. They can also cause a person to serve a sentence called marriage for the rest of his or her life. Many spouses serving a "marital sentence" live in silent, lonely desperation.

I am not an advocate of divorce, but frequently I wonder and empathize with those who appear to be the victims of terminally ill marriages or ones that died before they were even born. Reality would teach those living in dead and dying marriages to seek help in bringing life and vitality to that marriage. If help is refused, the death sentence will merely be lived out. Seeking help is always an option, but it takes two people working on the marriage to make the results effective and permanent.

Help, when it is sought, always takes time. Too many husbands and wives expect instant, miraculous solutions to barriers and problems that have existed in their marriage for many years.

There is no quick fix. There are only three options for a terminally ill marriage: seek help, let it continue to erode, or leave it. I believe the best choice is always an honest attempt by both parties to seek help in bringing new life and hope to the marriage. The real tragedy is that too few choose this alternative. Many times it will take more courage to try to heal a fractured relationship than to leave it.

These are the tough choices that tender people have to make!

12
Children Living in Step

In a previous chapter, I stated that there are several groupings of people who must live within or deal with a remarriage. The primary and secondary adults form the first group, followed by primary and secondary children. Primary and secondary relative structures form the third group, with community support systems for both groups coming in fourth. A remarriage will mix some if not all of those groupings together. The group that often has the most difficult time adjusting to remarriage is the children. A United States census statistic says that 7 million children were living in stepfamilies in 1985. A third of all children born in the eighties will live with a stepparent before they turn eighteen.

Since children have no vote and little say in any remarriage, they fall into the role of either insiders or outsiders. Emotionally, they form two groups: the excited, accepting, and cooperative versus the angry, confused, indifferent, and rebellious. If you currently have children living in a remarriage or about-to-be remarriage, what category would they fall into? If they are in the second grouping, they will be planting land mines everywhere you go in your new marriage.

Seldom do adults view remarriage from a child's perspective. Adults look at the gain while children more often look at the loss. Adults are excited about a new partner and new beginnings while children often mourn the death of their dearest dream—that somehow their primary parents would get back together and life would again be as it was. A remarriage of one or both of their parents is a death knell to their hope. When hope dies, a bitter spirit can take control and cause daily disruptions. There are no statistics available on how many second marriages are destroyed by children, but I would venture a guess that the numbers are high.

A report in *Newsweek* states, "Psychologists say that, as a group, stepchildren have more developmental, emotional and behavioral problems than children in intact families" (*Newsweek*, Special Edition, Winter-Spring 1990). Children of all ages are affected by divorce and remarriage. The response has a lot to do with the age of the child and the individual situation. Here are some general principles and guidelines that may be helpful:

1. Small children often make the best adjustment to a stepparent. They are more resilient and have not formed all their feelings and responses as older children have. If a primary parent abandons a child, that child may quickly attach himself or herself to the new stepparent. Surrogate love is better than rejection and no love at all. If a child has a healthy relationship with both primary and stepparent, he will feel more of a sense of belonging in a second family and will cause fewer problems. Love and acceptance go a long way in stepfamilies.

2. *Junior high and senior high children are less adjustable to a second marriage.* They are moving toward their own independence and want parents as supportive people rather than controlling people. In any new situation with older children, everyone tests the waters to see who is in control and just how much control they have. Older children want the security of home and parents along with a sense of growing freedom. For them, a new home structure throws security and freedom into question. If they cannot adjust to it, they may look for an early exit and feel they can never return.

3. *Grown children who are married and have children of their own are having increasing problems accepting the remarriage of their parents.* Older children have a sense of still wanting and needing a "home to go home to" at different times. For some, it is the old street address and the house they grew up in. For others, it is more the people than the address. Who do you go home to when both your mother and father have remarried, moved to a different area of the country, and have absorbed an entire other family system into their lives? Where do you fit? Where do they fit? Did the home and family you once knew dissolve into thin air?

Many of us are still testing that often-repeated line, "You can't go home again!" Home, whether in memory or in geography, represents security, stability, belonging, and identity. Divorce replaces the memory with a wound that remarriage can seldom heal for older children.

Married children with their own children are faced with explaining the divorce of their children's grandparents. Grandparents just aren't supposed to get divorced. When they do, it not only affects their children but also their grandchildren.

Older children have years of memory and history with their parents. Unless they have built a secure life of their own, their stability can be destroyed overnight. Bringing new stepparents into their lives, even at a distance, is difficult if not impossible. When you are thirtysomething, a new stepparent might be just another adult in your life.

Attitudes Determine Healthy Relationships

Children moving into a stepparent relationship have one of three attitudes toward that relationship. They may want it badly and they can't wait for it to become a reality. That attitude doesn't mean there will be no adjustment problems. It simply says the children are open to the relationship and excited by it. A second attitude is that they are opposed to it and don't want any part of it. If forced to be a part of it, they will remain outsiders and cause trouble for the new marriage. The third attitude is one of ambivalence or indifference. The children see themselves as totally unimportant to the situation. They have no sense of belonging. Older teens who are about ready to leave home often have this attitude. They have nothing invested and nothing to lose.

The attitude a child carries into the new family structure will in part determine his or her place in it. It will also dictate the responses from the adults involved.

Many children are denied the right to slowly form a relationship with a potential stepparent. The rebuff, "I married your mother, not you," may raise a barrier of hurt and anger. Children who feel discarded will not have a healthy attitude toward a stepparent. One bad attitude colliding with another will weaken the marital fabric.

You Cannot Force Relationships

Someone recently asked me, "Are there more happy than unhappy stepparent-child relationships?" I hope so, but I tend to see more of the unhappy ones because that is the area I work in. You cannot force happiness any more than you can force relationships. Some stepchildren will have good relationships with their stepparents and some will not. Your desire can be high and your effort supreme, but like marriage, it takes cooperation by everyone. For both hidden and revealed reasons, some relationships will never happen. When they do not, all you can do is be patient.

Many stepchildren choose not to build relationships with their stepparents for fear that any rejection they received from primary parents may reoccur. Rejection sends children into hiding. Pain will send them inside themselves and raise big walls to protect them. Many stepchildren are still running from the experiences they had with primary parents. Often, stepparents don't understand that and feel it must be something they have done or not done.

Building bridges is the best remover of walls in a relationship. It takes time and healthy experiences to build those bridges. One of the ways a stepparent can build bridges to a stepchild is through understanding what that child has walked through prior to entering this new relationship. The child's past can have a strong bearing on the present and future of the new home. The best way to deal with a child's bad memories is through understanding, time, and a willingness to build new and happier memories.

Sometimes a stepparent wants instant acceptance and respect from a stepchild when, in the child's opinion, he or she has not earned it. The more it is demanded, the less the chance of ever getting it. That is also true when a child wants instant affection and love from the new stepparent and does not receive it. Both deal with the unfulfilled expectations I spoke of earlier.

Early on, family forums should become part of a second marriage. During these times, expectations can be shared by all concerned. When certain family members don't live up to those expectations, reasons need to be explored. Everyone should have the freedom to express their feelings. Repressed feelings force children into becoming outsiders in a second marriage. Feelings are neither right nor wrong—they just are! Healthy children and adults learn to say, "I feel. . . ." Healthy second marriages are a place where feelings can be shared, judgments withheld, and growth encouraged.

In her popular book *Second Chances*, Judith Wallerstein states that seven things happen to a child when the primary family structure collapses. As I look over the list, I would say that all seven things are sometimes a part of a child's struggles when a second marriage takes place.

1. Fear is the first emotion a child feels at the collapse of a home. Fear might well be the same emotion a child feels when a parent is about to remarry—fear of the unknown, fear of the new person and situation, fear of new family members, fear of moving to a new home or city, fear of losing old friends, fear of everything and anything.

2. *Rejection by one parent or even both in a family-structure collapse is a fear that can quickly become a reality.* I have seen children in the postdivorce world rejected by a parent. After that rejection is experienced, the fear is easily transferred to a later stepparent relationship, even though there may be nothing to warrant it.

Listen to these powerful feelings expressed by a teenage friend who experienced a divorce in her family:

Hello. Is it you?
How do I know you won't be like the last—
    and leave like the last?
Will you really be there—
    when it's cold or when I'm scared?
Will you be the one to catch me when I fall,
    to let me cry and feel my pain?
Will you laugh and hold my hand as if to say,
    "I'm here and I will always be."
Can you take the time to get to know me
    and learn to love me?
Will you leave the busy day behind and share my life with me,
    and let me share yours with you?
Will your arms always be open to my yearning embrace?
Will you let me cry when the whole world is my enemy?
And will you hold me just as tight
    when the world is within my grasp?
Will you be proud of the person I have become?
It's sad, you know, for you weren't there to see me grow.
You weren't there to bandage my wounds or the broken hearts
    and dreams of my childhood.

For all you know is the person I am now.
The last one was there, you know.
He saw me fall as he turned and walked away.
So the father that helped create me
    was never really my Dad.
Is that who you will be?

Jennifer Dillon, 1989

3. Anger is the third emotion Dr. Wallerstein says children experience through a divorce. That anger may come from their inability to change the current situation. It can be directed at the people they feel could change the situation. It can be directed at all adults, including teachers, employers, and authority figures. Anger is also carried over into a stepparent structure, even though the stepparent did nothing to cause the anger. Anger in a second marriage can be directed at the primary parent in that marriage. There is probably nothing tougher to deal with than an angry child, regardless of age.

4. Powerlessness follows close behind anger because one often causes the other. Anger is being out of control. Powerlessness is knowing you have no control. Earlier, we established that children were the powerless people in any divorce. Unless they are allowed to control everything by their actions in a second marriage, they will again feel powerless. An angry, powerless child in a situation he or she does not want to be in can bring a quick end to a second marriage.

The strong and volatile emotions a child feels cannot be denied or excused. They cannot be carried along into a new family structure in the hope that structure will cause them to disappear. They must be dealt with *prior* to the establishment of that home.

5. *The first four emotions result in the fifth one: loneliness.* Actions and emotions that are out of control result in either isolation or toxic friendships with those in similar settings. Loneliness happens when you cut others off from your life for any reason. It also happens when they cut you off. We live in an age of increasing loneliness. People reach for all the false antidotes to resolve their loneliness when the real answer lies in building right relationships with God, yourself, and those around you.

Divorce often terminates what were considered good and healthy relationships. It even terminates what might have been bad relationships. Unless new, fulfilling relationships are built by the children in a new family, loneliness will dominate. It cannot be cured by new places, new diversions, or new excitements. It can be cured only by allowing people to bring meaning and wholeness to one's life. Loneliness says, "I feel I don't belong anywhere." Wholeness says, "I belong . . . and others belong to me."

6. *Loyalty is sought from the children by both divorcing parents.* Adults in divorce sometimes force the children into playing ridiculous games in the name of loyalty. Divorce seems to dictate that someone is right and someone is wrong and one must line up on the side of right if one is a child. The loyalty war is seldom won and can go on for years. In a stepfamily situation, the number of players increases, causing the war to escalate. Children are increasingly frustrated by the pressures that never seem to go away. If peer pressure is difficult for a child to handle, adult loyalty pressure is worse.

A word to the wise: Don't subject your children to this game. Nobody ever really wins, and most certainly, the child loses.

7. *A child feels guilt over the collapse of the family structure.* Some of that guilt comes from the child's inability to fix what went wrong. Some of it results when a child feels he or she was a cause for the parents' divorce. If that guilt is not dealt with when parents divorce, it can pile up and be transferred to the new family structure.

When guilt accumulates in the life of an adult or a child, it soon becomes an emotional prison from which escape seems impossible. The best release from guilt is found in forgiveness. Sometimes there has to be a therapeutic working through of guilt and forgiveness with all family members before a second marriage has any hope of lasting. Forgiveness is letting go and being set free to move on without being followed by dark clouds.

Most of us will always battle the threads of guilt in our lives. Guilt grows on the *shoulds* we all face. Release from that guilt is knowing we have choices; some will be right and some wrong, but we need not be condemned by them. Every marriage failure is shrouded in *shoulds*. Second marriages for adults and children need to be encased in the rainbow of the words, *I can!*

These seven emotions may not be experienced by children in an orderly progression. As an adult, you need to be aware of what feelings are present, and then take the time and effort to deal with them. They can be turned into places of growth for everyone, or they can become seedbeds of destruction for both the children and the adults in a second marriage.

Ask your children *how they feel* about the failure of the first marriage and the prospect of a second marriage. Give them time and space for the processing of those feelings. Remember, they have experienced the same loss as you. Let them know the feelings they have are okay.

13
Watching for the Warning Signs

There are always indicators to a troubled marriage. The warning signs are either paid attention to or denied. Denial may not mean the imminent failure of the marriage but merely the shifting into another marriage gear called "fight or flight." Unless divorced people recognize the reasons their first marriage failed and learn from those reasons, their vision in a second marriage may not be any better. The people who don't learn anything from a first-marriage failure are the people who don't look deep enough.

When I counsel newly divorced people, I usually ask why they feel their marriage failed. Most of the reasons they give run along these lines: "He [she] had a mid-life crisis"; "He [she] ran off with another person"; "He [she] said he didn't love me anymore." These are real reasons, but I always want to ask what was happening *before* the reasons became reality. As illustrated earlier in the Divorce Time Line, marriages don't self-destruct overnight. It takes months, even years, as things build to an explosive or silent and desperate end.

Some of the indications that a second marriage is in trouble may be the same as in a first marriage. Others will be relevant only to a second marriage. Keep your eyes open for the following situations.

The Children Have Taken Over

I have a friend whose favorite saying is, "Never surrender leadership." Many parents who are living with stepchildren and primary children in a second marriage would do well to remember that. Lack of discipline, indecision, and inability to give direction are the three basic causes for adults losing leadership in a second marriage. As the conflict increases, parents are tempted to go into hiding and let the children do as they please. Once that leadership is lost, it can seldom be reclaimed.

In a second marriage where children are involved, there will always be a leadership seesaw between noncustodial primary parents and resident parents. Seldom will everyone work together smoothly for the same ends. An absentee parent loses leadership and a resident parent assumes it. When the resident parent gives up leadership, the children take control and seeds of marital destruction can be planted. Children will always test the waters to see who is in charge. They frequently use one set of parents against the other to achieve their own goals.

Expectations Have Soured

Most people get in trouble when their expectations are either too high or too low. In an earlier chapter, I addressed the issue of failed expectations and listed some of them. It is important to spot them in advance before they begin to contribute to the decline of a relationship.

Shattered expectations are often stockpiled as they occur and hauled out only when needed as battle tools. As one comic quipped, "People become hysterical, then they become historical."

Mood and temperament changes in an individual are often indicators that the barometer of feeling is climbing. If those changes go unrecognized or unchallenged, they may cause strong negative feelings to grow between a husband and wife.

Lack of positive effort in the building of a new relationship may be a warning sign of failed expectations. The "why try" attitude usually means, "I tried and was disappointed that you didn't." Two people can work hard at building a new relationship until the wedding takes place and a new life begins. Then, one or the other ceases to invest major effort in continuing the growth. How often have you heard the line, "He [she] has changed since we got married." People who are awake and alert can spot those changes taking place and try to do something about them. Expectations sour gradually. You can observe the warning signs and get help.

155

It Seems You've Been Here Before

When your second marriage takes on all the appearances and similarities of your first marriage, look out! The warning light is on, and you will probably handle things the same way you did in your first marriage. Growing feelings of sameness are indicators that your marriage may be headed down the wrong road. When in discussions and arguments you use the same words, actions, and attempted resolutions used in the first marriage, trouble may be brewing. Watch the patterns that are developing and work to break them.

The two people in my office each felt the other was the reincarnation of their former spouse. Both had been married previously to highly dysfunctional persons but had chosen their own ways to cope. Those methods were so entrenched in their lives that they were now using the same ones to deal with their new spouse. When issues great or small came up in the new marriage, the old tools of combat came out and were used for attempts at resolution.

It is not easy to break the habits of a thirty-year marriage and realize that your new mate is not a clone of your former one.

Frayed Finances

Money, or lack of it, still seems to be at the heart of most marital problems. If first marriages cost money, second marriages cost more, for there are always carrying charges. Financial resentments toward primary-family responsibilities can build month by month. When you need the money that is going elsewhere and the money you should receive is not coming in, tension will begin to build and resentment will follow. Pretty soon there will be good guys and bad guys and the marital relationship will be endangered. Early in this book I asked the question, "Can you afford a second marriage?" My counseling experience tells me few give this much thought. They just remarry and apply for new credit cards!

When financial frustrations begin to surface, don't let them build. They can become seeds of destruction in a second marriage. Budgets, long-range planning, and an honest recognition of financial responsibilities in a second marriage will keep you from falling victim to frayed finances.

Growing Apart or Growing Together?

It is relatively easy for two people to live together and grow apart. Many first marriages terminate for that reason. By the time the divorce happens, there is little feeling involved because both parties have spent years distancing themselves from each other. Many people live their entire marriage this way and never divorce. Each of them go their separate ways and compromise on the times they need to be together for public appearances. Both of those conditions are sad and result when people are not really aware of the growing-apart process.

In today's culture, drifting apart is a simple process. When both work at different jobs and have a few different social commitments and a couple of children with their agendas tossed in, there is little time left for a bond to grow between them. It's like sitting on a raft when the tide is going out. Suddenly, you are a long way from shore, but you have not noticed the distance or even felt the movement.

Two people can grow apart very quickly in a second marriage. There are more demands and divisions of time. There is more ground to cover and more people demanding a part of your time. When the emotional space between two people is not filled, one of two things will happen: either the space will become larger or someone else will fill it.

Growing apart is almost a silent cause of the death of a second marriage. The prevention is spending quality time together as husband and wife. There are many ways to accomplish that. It just has to be done. Quality time, quality sharing, quality planning, and quality conversation all go together. When none of those is happening, the warning light is on!

A Former Spouse Is Ruining Your Second Marriage

Someone has said, "The only difference between death and divorce is that in divorce you have to keep dealing with the corpse." I am certain that some second marriages have been destroyed by the invading specter of a former spouse. Some important questions a person must face when entering a second marriage are:

- Can I live with my new mate's former spouse just over the horizon?
- Will having that person around the edges of my new marriage affect the relationship in a negative way?
- Will he [she] keep grinding my new spouse down with problems that are never resolved?
- Will he [she] constantly disrupt the lives of my children or stepchildren?

The role ex-spouses play prior to your marriage will probably intensify after the marriage. Causing conflict in the lives of other people can be great revenge. There are a hundred different variations of games former spouses play with present spouses. There is nothing that will cause more unrest in a second marriage than a vindictive former spouse seeking varied forms of revenge.

The warning signs of former-spouse intervention can be observed even before the second marriage. If your current spouse runs to his or her former spouse whenever demands are made, it may seem acceptable prior to your remarriage and excusable as just wrapping up things from the past. However, when it happens frequently in your new marriage, allegiance will be brought into question and resentment may build. Unresolved resentment is a warning sign that the foundation of your new marriage is being shaken.

Family Structures Can Cause Conflict

If a former spouse can affect the outcome and happiness of a second marriage, the former spouse's family may not be far behind. The rising issue of grandparents' rights alone can put pressure on a new family. The more involved the remarriage is structurally, the more people there will be vying for the children's time and offering their advice on the creation of a new family. The acceptance or rejection of your new mate by your own primary family structure can be crucial to the success of your new marriage. When your new spouse is rejected and your former spouse still accepted, you will find the waters of remarriage stormy.

A great deal of the possible conflict in a second marriage can come from the extended family forces. The pressure they exert can become unbearable and easily destroy the foundation of a second marriage. Moving away from family forces is sometimes the only salvation. One should not have to run from family, but when they cause constant conflict in your remarriage, you had better call the movers!

Family structures are as intricate as emotions in individuals. Some are exclusive while others are inclusive. Some are more accepting while others are rejecting. Some are loving and some are cruel. Family structures, like children, are part of the carrying charges in a second marriage.

Many sons and daughters want to defend their primary family unit to the death, regardless of what they do, think, or say. When that is done to the exclusion of your new spouse, he or she will not be around for too many family gatherings. If one is unacceptable to a family structure before a second marriage, there is no guarantee that person will be more acceptable after the marriage takes place.

A few words of advice on family structures: Take a long, hard look at the structure you are marrying into *before* you remarry. The dynamic you observe will be the one you inherit. If you never gave it much thought prior to your wedding and that structure is now giving you problems within your marriage, get some outside help in the form of counseling. You may have to take some hard stands to preserve your marriage, and outside guidance can help firm up that stand. Toxic interpersonal family dynamics can choke the life out of a second marriage very quickly. There are usually too many people to deal with, and when they are all on the other side, you want to run away and hide.

New family structures seldom blend easily. It takes work, time, understanding, and patience. Remember, they have had many years to perfect their idiosyncrasies prior to your arrival. Good ones will enhance your marriage a thousandfold. Bad ones will either scuttle it or send you looking for a private island in the Caribbean with a NO VISITORS sign out front.

Transferring Dysfunctions Can Be Harmful to Your Marriage

Today, there is a tremendous amount of attention given to the dysfunctional family. Books list the many dysfunctions by categories. Family members are sent back into the past to seek out dysfunctions and try to correct them. In growing numbers, people are told that the problems they have today are the result of living in a dysfunctional family.

Every five years or so, we come up with a new catchphrase or word that serves as an emotional vacuum cleaner for our struggles. The truth is that there are many families that don't function at the proper level to provide the nurturing a family should provide. I believe most families are sound and nourishing, that none is perfect, and all have to deal with dysfunctions from time to time. Correcting dysfunctions once they have been identified in any structure is difficult and tedious work.

The crisis of divorce often brings buried problems in a person to the surface. Some were inherited, some created. Both need to be dealt with to set the person free and allow wholeness in his or her life. Many of the early struggles in people's lives that have been buried for years tend to resurface at a time of hurt or dramatic change.

Increasingly, counselors and therapists are discovering that dysfunctions in birth families are often passed along through its members to new families. Dysfunctions that have been repressed and not dealt with for many years may be manifested in the new family. It is only as these dysfunctions surface and are acknowledged that help can be received. Dysfunctions that are denied or remain buried are simply passed along from family to family without hope of resolution and breaking the chains of dysfunction.

At any point of major change in your life, it is always wise to take a long, hard look at yourself. Ask yourself the following questions:

- Who am I now?
- What caused me to be what I am?
- What have I been living with that is unhealthy?
- How can I resolve the unresolved in my life?
- How do I get rid of the excess baggage I have been carrying around for many years?
- How do I process healing and forgiveness?
- Is it time to air my repressions and find answers?

Those are hard questions to ask oneself and harder still to begin working on. If those and similar questions are not faced when one marriage ends and another is about to begin, you may simply transfer the past dysfunctions of your life to a new stage surrounded by a new audience. If those dysfunctions contributed to the failure of your first marriage, they may perform an even quicker execution of your second marriage.

Wholeness in another person cannot be discerned by some emotional x-ray process. People with severe dysfunctions may appear whole, hold responsible jobs, make healthy salaries, and speak intelligently. Some dysfunctions are buried only inches below the surface and appear at very unexpected times. Others are buried deep and remain hidden from view.

When you have lived with another person's dysfunctions, you can become suspicious of every person you meet. You may always wonder what is just below the surface.

None of us is responsible for "fixing" another person, even though frequently we would like to try. We are only responsible to fix ourselves and discover who we really are under the layers of our protective armor.

Dysfunctions in families involve relationships. If those relationships continue to be unhealthy, they will be perpetuated in a continuing string of families. The ones you lived through came from somewhere, and the danger is that you may take them down the road with you. Dysfunctional chains must be broken if there is to be health in a second marriage. Counseling and therapy are often needed to assist in severe situations. Remember, the word is *resolution*, not transfer!

Help! I Lost My Space

For most people, remarriage means changing living situations. Some people with children marry others with children. Some without children marry others with children. Some without children marry others without children and give birth to new children. Still others have grown children out on their own and marry someone with children still living at home. The blended family can involve some varied mixes. On a very basic level, it can mean new and different living conditions with numerical changes in the people living with you. Few blended families live in as much harmony as the TV residents of "The Brady Bunch." Whenever I watched that show and saw the apparent size of the house they lived in, I wondered where they all slept, ate, played, etc. They always appeared crowded but blissfully happy.

What happens in a second marriage when you wake up one morning and realize you have either lost your space or your space has been invaded? Your warning light may go on as you begin to resent the new way you have chosen to live. If your children leave for a weekend with their other parent while your new spouse's children invade your home for two days of chaos, you may find yourself sneaking away to the crawl space above the garage just to have some space to yourself.

Having a place of quiet and privacy is important to the balance in all of our lives. It is little wonder that older people, who have served in the trenches of parenthood for many years, relish the joys of peace and tranquillity in their homes after the children leave.

It is in our "space" of quiet and seclusion that we find the strength to eventually walk back into the daily combat of life. We read in Psalm 46:10 RSV, "Be still, and know that I am God." David the Psalmist found that God is often most present when things are most quiet.

There are many forms of being crowded in life. We each need our space from that crowdedness. Second marriages are no exception. Many of my second-marriage friends have confessed their need for and struggle to find some space for themselves in their new marriages. That does not mean the marriages are falling apart. It just means that we need to give each other the gift of space in order to regroup and return to the front lines each day.

When claustrophobia strikes in a second marriage, seek your place of renewal and sanctuary. The place of peace is a gift that everyone in the family needs from time to time. Sometimes closing the door to your room can afford the peace you need. At other times it will be sending the family off on a camping trip while you enjoy the solitude at home. For a husband and wife, it may mean a trip to an out-of-town hotel for the weekend.

Silence, solitude, and seclusion are always gifts that renew and refresh us. From them we gain the strength to go another mile in the journey through life.

Questions and Suggestions

There are hundreds of questions about the many aspects of remarriage. In this section, I want to focus on some that are frequently asked and make some suggestions that come out of my counseling experience in the divorce-recovery field. Bear in mind that there are exceptions to every situation, but the exceptions are usually in the minority.

Q. Should everyone wait two to three years after a divorce before they remarry?

S. It depends on the kind of divorce a person goes through. Many marriages die long, slow deaths while others end suddenly. In the slow-death kind, a person may make the growth-and-survival adjustments before the divorce is final. Some people even bring a form of closure to a relationship they are still living in before the divorce is enacted. The basic question is how much homework needs to be done before you are ready for remarriage. Sudden divorces demand much more homework than the slow-death variety.

Q. What happens when you know you need more time to grow prior to a remarriage, but the person you are building a relationship with is pushing you toward remarriage because he or she has been divorced a long time and feels ready for it?

S. Tell the person you cannot be pushed and need the time to grow that he or she had. If he loves and respects your needs, he will give you that time. If he won't, perhaps you had better back away from the relationship. Using pressure is no way to begin building a second marriage.

Q. Is it right to do some checking around on a person with whom you have a serious relationship?

S. Yes, because serious relationships lead to remarriage, and that other person may reveal about himself or herself only what he or she wants you to know. It may sound strange, but I often recommend a financial check. You may be surprised at what you are told compared with what you find out. Remember, people coming from hurting situations are most vulnerable. There is a willing rescuer around every corner.

Q. Is there a big difference between marrying someone who has lost a mate by death and one who has lost a mate by divorce?

S.   Yes. Sometimes the one who has lost a mate by death wants to enshrine that person forever in heart and home and refuses to allow the new mate into that space. The new mate fights a never-ending battle of putting memories to rest and combating constant comparisons with the deceased mate. This usually appears in the dating process, but love can blind you to its consequences.

Q.   Should you enter a second marriage when your children are opposed to it?

S.   First, listen to their reasons and think about their validity. They may see warning lights that you are avoiding in the name of love. Second, find out if your best friends share the same feelings and ask why. Third, if the opposing children live with you and will live within this new setting, you can be assured there will be endless conflict if the marriage takes place. When you love someone, you want them to be accepted by the ones you love. If that is not forthcoming, life can be tumultuous. People in this situation must decide what they are giving away and what they are gaining.

Q.   Can a marriage work if one partner has children and the other has never been married?

S.   Yes, but it means a major adjustment for all involved parties. The single person gives up a "do what I want when I want to" life-style. The single parent must understand it will take a long time for their different life-styles to merge. Children in this kind of remarriage are often looked upon as nuisances rather than family by the never-married-before spouse.

169

Q. What about changing the last name of your children to the surname of your new spouse?

S. Since this applies only to the woman's children, it can be a topic that causes conflict unless resolved early. A legal process is involved in having a child's name changed. The primary father must also give consent. If consent is not given, the name change may not be approved by the court. A general rule of thumb is that once a child has reached school age, it is too late to tack a new last name onto them. There are often strong feelings about last names. Even the death of a father when a child is an infant followed by a subsequent remarriage doesn't make it simpler. Grandparents can get absorbed in this conflict as well. Children themselves have strong feelings. There is no right and wrong here. Sometimes it has to be talked out with the help of a wise counselor who can help those involved look at all sides.

Q. How do you deal with a remarriage family structure that refuses to accept you as a new member of that unit?

S. There is little you can do about rejection by another person. Even your spouse, who is related to that family unit, is often powerless that the family does not accept his or her choice of a new spouse. If support systems cannot be built within a family, they must be built outside it. Sometimes it takes years for acceptance to come from a new family. Sometimes it never comes. As you go into the relationship, you need to ask yourself if you can live with that. If not, end the relationship before it becomes a remarriage.

Q. Should you meet your new spouse's children prior to remarriage, even if they live on the other side of the country with the former spouse?

S. Yes, yes, and yes! Wherever they live and however old they are, they will become part of your life. Geographically removed children cannot be hidden away forever. If they are under eighteen, you will probably have them as seasonal houseguests. They might even come to live with you permanently. You had better get to know them *before* you remarry. They could become your carrying charges!

Q. Is it proper for a second-marriage ceremony to take place in a church with all the trappings customarily included in a first marriage?

S. I believe it is. A second-marriage ceremony can and perhaps should be different from a first-marriage ceremony. I like to see the children included in this ceremony because two family units are being joined together. Second-marriage ceremonies take careful planning as they can anger many peripheral family members. A second marriage need not be hidden away in a roadside wedding chapel in Las Vegas. It can and should be a celebration as well as a commitment.

Q. Are second marriages biblically correct?

S. This question is well worth asking. Dr. Dwight Small's book *Remarriage and God's Renewing Grace*, listed under Resources at the back of this book, provides great help in this area.

Q. What do you do with the problem of children bouncing back and forth from stepparent family to primary-parent family?

S.   Children have a way of testing a new structure. If they don't like it, you may hear the line, "I want to go live with my mother [father]." When living with that other parent becomes a problem, they want to return to you. You can live with yo-yo kids for only so long. Either your string will break or theirs will. Continuity must be established for growth to take place. You can afford one revolution of the parental merry-go-round. After that, decisions must be made and carried out.

Q.   How do you deal with stepchildren who, when they come to live with you, won't abide by your rules?

S.   You and your new spouse need to have a long talk and decide that you are very together in rules, regulations, and discipline. Guest or permanent-resident children have to be given the option of living with your standards or living elsewhere.

Q.   What happens when a long-lost former spouse reappears in the lives of your children and wants life to be "wonderful" again?

S.   Few former spouses totally vanish from the face of the earth. However, many of them have a habit of popping up at inopportune times and causing unrest, mostly with the children. Since you and that person are divorced and your children are not divorced from that person, they have to decide what the relationship will be. Let it be the problem of your children and former spouse. When there is a strong stepparent bonding, it will be difficult for the children to relate to a parent who has been absent from their lives for many years.

Q.   What kind of pre-second-marriage counseling is needed?

S. Several recommended tests for those contemplating a second marriage are listed under Resources at the back of this book. A qualified counselor can administer them and talk over the results with both parties. They are indicators of factors that often don't appear in a forming relationship. They will show high or low levels of marital compatibility. *Anyone entering a second marriage should have all the tests and counseling possible prior to that marriage.*

Q. Should you take your children along if you have a second-marriage honeymoon?

S. Only if you don't want your new spouse to come along!

Q. How do you tell your children that you are planning to marry the person you have been dating for many months?

S. Gently and with love. Talk to them about your need for someone special in your life after they have grown and moved on. Assure them that they will be a vital part of this new relationship. Don't leave them outside, even if they are older and living on their own. In most situations, it is the responsibility of the primary parent, not the potential stepparent, to tell the children. If the children live at home, it would be wise to do it with the proposed stepparent absent. This enables the children to make any response they want without someone getting hurt. This can be a really tough time or a wonderfully celebrative time. There are no guarantees.

Q. If you remarry and already have several children of your own and choose to give birth to new children in your second marriage, where will those new children fit in the already-formed family structures?

S.   The immediate-family unit is easiest to integrate new children into. It is much tougher to make them feel they belong to the surrounding structures such as former in-law grandparents, former spouse structure, aunts, uncles, cousins, and so on. Your prior children have a history while the new children have only the history they are creating in the new structure. They often feel left out of some things unless everyone makes them feel included.

Q.   Are prenuptial agreements wise, or do they tend to invalidate trust?

S.   In many instances, they are wise. If you have inherited money or have money set aside for your children's education, it is wise to separate this from your marriage by legal means. If a person feels you do not trust him or her because you are doing this, you might wonder if you should trust him or her at all. I counsel people contemplating second marriages to look at this carefully. It also helps relax your primary family if they know you are taking care of a possible inheritance. In today's world of changing divorce laws, it has become wise business.

Q.   What about separate bank accounts?

S.   I feel this is different from prenuptial agreements. It has more to do with the practical day-to-day money management of a family. If you are getting married with a hundred thousand dollars in your bank account, you may not want a joint account. All forms of money management should be talked about and worked through *prior* to a second marriage.

Q. Is it possible to remain friends with your former spouse after you enter a second marriage?

S. Yes, two people did it in 1953. In all seriousness, it really depends whether or not the two former spouses want that and how comfortable a new spouse feels with it. It is certainly easier to be friends than enemies, and it makes life much easier for the children as well.

Q. Should a new spouse stay out of the conflicts his or her mate has with a former spouse?

S. For the most part, yes! When conflicts between your mate and his or her former spouse become your wars, it will begin to upset the balance of your marriage. This kind of agreement should be made prior to a second marriage and held to rigidly afterward. Problems between former spouses create one of the great second-marriage conflict zones. Make every effort to stay out of that zone.

Q. What should you do if your present spouse tries to involve you in his or her struggles with a former spouse?

S. Go to your room and watch "Cosby." His family never has those kind of problems.

The "Am I Ready for Remarriage?" Test

1. Have I forgiven my former spouse as well as myself?
2. Have I experienced a healing of hurts caused by my divorce?
3. Am I still playing "get even" games with my former spouse?
4. When someone asks me about my divorce, do I have a hard time recalling events and situations?
5. Do I think of myself as a divorced person?
6. Has my self-esteem grown measurably over the past three years?
7. Do I enjoy my work?
8. Do people tell me they can't believe how well I'm doing?

9. Am I always looking for a potential mate?
10. Would I rather go out with others than by myself?
11. Am I haunted by loneliness?
12. Do I enjoy making decisions?
13. Am I glad there is no one there when I come home at the end of the day?
14. Do I enjoy going to singles groups?
15. Do I resent the word *single?*
16. Am I envious when I see happily married people?
17. Can I measure my growth in the three years since I became single again?
18. Am I looking for someone to take care of me?
19. Am I looking for someone to take care of?
20. Do I feel that the person I remarry has to be accepted and liked by my children and family?
21. Do I enjoy hearing other people's divorce war stories?
22. Do I believe I will make a good wife or husband for someone?
23. Do I still largely fear remarriage?
24. Do I feel comfortable with my singleness?
25. Am I excited about possible career advancements or changes?
26. Do I usually wait for someone to tell me what to do?
27. Am I angry that I am single at this point in my journey through life?
28. Am I still bitter about my divorce?
29. Do I feel good about my personal growth and accomplishments?
30. Do I make plans and work toward goals in my life?
31. Do I think all men (women) have a hidden agenda in remarriage?

32. Do I believe I am lovable?
33. Do I believe I can be a contributor to the happiness of someone else?
34. Am I a happy person?
35. Do I believe that God really loves me and has forgiven me for my divorce regardless of what other people might think?
36. Is my life-style mergeable?
37. Do I have a "who needs you" feeling toward the opposite sex?
38. Is the thought of remarriage an exciting challenge?
39. Am I willing to invest a year or two in building a relationship that could lead to marriage?
40. Would I feel safe with a prenuptial agreement?
41. Have I worked through my biblical concerns about the issue of remarriage?
42. Can I live happily ever after if I do not choose remarriage?
43. Do I believe there is only one person out there for me, and if I miss him (her), that's it?
44. Do I believe I am a loser if a long-term relationship does not end in marriage?
45. Have I traded in my "Happiness Is Being Single" shirt for one that says, "Happiness Is Being Human"?
46. Have I grown in my relationship with God? Is He real and vital in my life?

Every test demands some sort of grade. We are always eager to know whether we passed or failed. If you answered the above questions according to what I have observed, you are well on the way to growing and being prepared for remarriage.

YES on 1, 2, 4, 6, 7, 8, 12, 14, 17, 20, 22, 24, 25, 29, 30, 32, 33, 34, 35, 36, 38, 39, 40, 41, 42, 45, 46.
NO on 3, 5, 9, 10, 11, 13, 15, 16, 18, 19, 21, 23, 26, 27, 28, 31, 37, 43, 44.

A word of caution: Please don't take your test results to the next singles meeting you attend and set a table by the door under a sign that says, "All offers gratefully considered!" If your score was good, just smile a lot and know you have grown!

A Second-Marriage Ceremony

The following wedding ceremony outline is credited to my friends Austin and Lynn Goodale. It is the most meaningful and scriptural second-marriage ceremony I have witnessed in over thirty years of ministry. This outline is intended only as a guide for those wondering how to make a second marriage significant to everyone involved.

PRELUDE MUSIC Piano background, joyful and light

CANDLE LIGHTING Special solo sung during lighting of candles

SEATING OF PARENTS Second special solo sung during seating

PROCESSIONAL Children of the bride process after attendants, bride on arm of oldest son

WELCOME BY OFFICIATING PASTOR TO FAMILY AND FRIENDS Wedding party on floor level here

PASTORAL PRAYER

PASTORAL EXPLANATION FOR BIBLICAL BASIS OF MARRIAGE

GIVING OF THE BRIDE   By oldest son, parent, or relative

WEDDING PARTY PROCEEDS TO SECOND LEVEL ON STEPS

SOLO   Bride and groom face each other during song

MARRIAGE VOWS EXCHANGED   Use those of presiding pastor or write your own

EXCHANGE OF RINGS   Use of rings explained by minister
Groom first, stating vows, followed by bride (these vows can also be written by bride and groom)

MOVE TO UPPER LEVEL OF PLATFORM BEFORE COMMUNION TABLE
Communion table is set up with two single slim candles lighted, one large candle between them, unlighted. Small loaf of bread and single silver chalice containing communion juice also on table

READING OF 1 CORINTHIANS CHAPTER 13   As bride and groom kneel before the table, children come to stand beside parents as they are called by name

INTRODUCTION OF COMMUNION BY PASTOR
Groom serves bride the bread, followed by the cup
Bride serves groom the bread, followed by the cup
Groom serves children who stand around the table

PRAYER OF BLESSING FOR THE BLENDED FAMILY BY PASTOR

SOLO   "We Are a Household of Faith"

LIGHTING OF THE SINGLE CANDLE BY GROOM AND BRIDE   Single candles are blown out and only large candle remains lighted

PASTOR EXPLAINS CANDLE LIGHTING SIGNIFICANCE

PASTOR PRONOUNCES BRIDE AND GROOM HUSBAND AND WIFE AS THEY FACE AUDIENCE

WEDDING PARTY MOVES TO FLOOR LEVEL   Pastor talks briefly about challenges and commitments to family—words of Ruth are used

FAMILY AND FRIENDS ARE INVITED TO COME FORWARD AND ENCIRCLE WEDDING PARTY BY HOLDING HANDS AND JOINING IN SINGING   "We Are One in the Bond of Love"

RECESSIONAL

Note: All wedding ceremonies should reflect the personal input and desires of the wedding party. Meaning and creativity are a vital part of the ceremony. If the participants have a deep and real faith in God, that should be reflected in the ceremony. The music should contribute to the overall meaning and not detract from it. In a second-wedding ceremony, the children should be involved. First weddings involve only two principal people. Second weddings involve children as well as family structures and support systems. It is a celebration. Make it celebrative!

Postscript

When you have finished reading this book, there are three things to remember:

1. Take the time for healing and closure after a marriage ends before you consider remarriage.
2. Do your homework before you remarry—all of it!
3. You need time and patience to build a second marriage.

In *Growing in Remarriage*, I have tried to address the issues that come up most frequently when I counsel remarried couples and those considering remarriage. If you have questions that remain unanswered, write to me at the address below and I will try to help you.

Jim Smoke
P.O. Box 24450
Tempe, Arizona 85282

Resources

Books

Bohannan, Paul. *All the Happy Families*. New York: McGraw-Hill Book Company, 1985.

Harley, Willard F., Jr. *His Needs, Her Needs*. Old Tappan, New Jersey: Fleming H. Revell Company, 1986.

Juroe, David and Bonnie. *Successful Stepparenting*. Old Tappan, New Jersey: Fleming H. Revell Company, 1983.

Richards, Dr. Larry. *Remarriage: A Healing Gift From God*. Dallas: WORD Incorporated, 1981.

Small, Dr. Dwight. *Remarriage and God's Renewing Grace*. Grand Rapids, Michigan: Baker Book House, 1986.

Smoke, Jim. *Living Beyond Divorce*. Eugene, Oregon: Harvest House Publishers, 1984.

Visher, John S. and Emily B. *Stepfamilies: A Guide to Working With Stepparents and Stepchildren.* New York: Bruner-Mazel, 1979.

Wallerstein, Dr. Judith, and Sandra Blakeslee. *Second Chances: Men, Women and Children a Decade After Divorce.* New York: Ticknor & Fields, 1989.

Psychological Tests

The following tests are familiar to most counselors. You may find them useful in second-marriage counseling.

Prepare and Enrich (available through P.O. Box 190, Minneapolis, Minnesota 55458)

Taylor Johnson Temperament Analysis

Meyers-Briggs Personality Indicator

Minnesota Multi-Phasic Inventory 2

16 PRF Personality Research Form

Marital Satisfaction Inventory